The Li..g ..p..

The Living Gospel

LUKE TIMOTHY JOHNSON

In association with *Priests and People*

continuum
LONDON • NEW YORK

Continuum

The Tower Building   15 East 26th Street
11 York Road   New York
London SE1 7NX   NY 10010

www.continuumbooks.com

First published 2004

British Library Cataloguing-in-Publication Data
A catalogue record for this book is available from the British Library.

ISBN 0-8264-7480-2

Typeset by RefineCatch Limited, Bungay, Suffolk
Printed and bound by Cromwell Press Ltd, Trowbridge, Wiltshire

Contents

Contents

Preface

Anthropologists use the term participant observer for the researcher who enters fully into the life of the tribe being studied, while retaining sufficient critical distance to make native ways intelligible to others. He's there but not entirely. This is a role I have played in Christian theology. I am at home here. I have studied it a bit, and I am concerned with the life of the church. In other ways, though, I am observer more than participant. My academic location is Bible rather than doctrinal or systematic theology, and because I am ex-monk/ex-priest, I am not fully an insider to Catholic conversations. The loss in position is however a gain in freedom, and I have always written – as an amateur, to be sure – in areas beyond my verifiable expertise.

This collection of essays represents a portion of the writing I have done for those outside the academy and my own (ever-narrowing) field of New Testament studies. When asked to pull them together with an eye to collection, I discovered that the pieces that might still be worth reading fell into three fairly clear groups: broadly theological essays, scriptural reflections, and Jesus. The topics naturally overlap. The division between theology and scripture is both artificial and unhelpful. One of my constant preoccupations has been how to read Scripture for the life of the church in a manner that is at once loving and critical, challenging yet charitable. And the figure of Jesus looms so large because, well, because he looms so large in scripture and theology! But I have written a lot on Jesus also because the controversy over the historical Jesus calls into question how we read scripture and how we think theologically.

These are short essays, mostly around three thousand words, which appeared in a variety of publications and were directed to specific circumstances and readers. They don't contain everything I think about each subject – I have written a few books and scholarly articles during the same time I was spinning off these short pieces – but they do contain my thinking in a concentrated and sometimes fresh form.

Although everything I write reveals its dependence on better minds than my own, I must express particular gratitude to four people. My former students at Yale Divinity School, David Heim (of *The Christian Century*) and Paul Baumann (of *Commonweal*) recruited me to write for a larger audience in their publications. Without the constant goading and encouragement of Paul Baumann, in particular, my life would have been less busy but also less interesting over the past decade. Many of the reviews in this collection were done for him and the readers of *Commonweal*.

And then there is David Sanders, O.P. Many of these essays began life in the British journal, *Priests and People*, of which he is editor. Once a year, David would write me a note, asking me to work up an essay on, oh, sin and suffering, or some other equally daunting subject, in three thousand words. And then he would print them! I grew to look forward to his next assignment, for I invariably found that I grew by having to think about new things. When I finally got to visit David and his fellow Dominicans at Blackfriars in Oxford, it was a delightful reward for a long-term and, until then, entirely literary relationship. Finally, I must thank Robin Baird-Smith, the Publishing Director of *Continuum* in the UK, for his interest in these short pieces and his encouragement in putting them together for publication, as well as Andrea Tucker, who helped me organize them.

No, I must thank still another, my dear wife Joy, who has been for me all these years not only the best example of what it means to be a true Christian but also the best and most loving partner through life.

Luke Timothy Johnson
January 15, 2004

Part One:

Theology of the Bible

Chapter 1

Theology and the Spiritual Life

When we think of the 'spiritual life,' we ought carefully to consider whose life it is of which we speak, and whose spirit. It makes a great difference. Are we speaking of the human activity of seeking perfection by piety and practice? Or, are we speaking of God's Life, which through the Holy Spirit is active in human existence?

If by the 'spiritual life' we mean the attempt to purify and control the impulsive human psyche by meditative technique; if perfection is regarded as the gradual etherealization of the body; if prayer is seen as the place where the body's demands are relativized by the governing principle of one's higher self; then, we do not sin by leaving such play to the dilettante and adept. If such sport does no great good, neither does it inflict great harm, except in some a terminal fuzziness. Not much rigour of thought is required, for there is no significant event: only the classic mechanism of fear, working itself out.

But if we understand by the spiritual life the implications for human attitudes and behavior of God's gift of life, then we need to be sharper and more alert. We have to do, not with the bland and predictable patterns of human compulsion, which tend toward a perfection of rigidity and truncation, but with the alien, surprising and awesome intrusion of the Holy into our lives, smashing our preconceptions and models of holiness alike with brutal calm.

If it is God with which we have to do, and not simply our idolatrous craving for perfection, then we need to think hard and well. We need to do theology, and quick, for this is a consuming fire, and those not devoured get scorched. Not now the sleepy tapes of soothing spiritual lullabies, and the restful repose of babes sated on spiritual milk. This is dangerous stuff. Who would dance with these flames need be nimble on the feet, for they move to their own music.

If we are called to attention by God's Life and Holy Spirit, then the 'spiritual life' is not a pleasant option we might like to pursue when we have space and time; it is that which is now creating its own space and time within us, and to neglect it is to lose ourselves. This is the implicit (and all the more real for that) nucleus of our entire theological enterprise. It is not a matter of *adiaphora* (like wanting to use incense or not, or wanting wider stoles); it is not a question of plastic deserts and make-believe solitude. When we are called to attention by the Holy, we are involved in idolatry and faith, sin and grace, slavery and freedom; within the tangled, complex and resistent fabric of our very lives.

If, as theologians, we have as our goal the rigorous and disciplined reflection on the Christian Mystery, we need to ask ourselves whether we can be content with just one or two or three voices being identified (by ourselves or by others) as the only ones interested in this reflection. If we are discontent with the substance or style of what is known in these parts as 'the spiritual life', then we are called (if it is truly God's Spirit with which we are concerned) to join together in clearer, harder, and more rigorous thought precisely on these matters, to examine and discern the issues, to separate out the Mystery from the mystification.

We might start by thinking, not about 'spiritual formation,' as a programme whose end we confidently know, and the steps of which we accurately can predict, but rather of 'being formed by the Spirit', as the continually fearful and attractive heart of our shared theological enterprise.

Such a centre and starting place for our thinking leads to pondering what it is we mean by theology. If we are to speak seriously about theology as an activity by which faith seeks articulation (both in praise, and in relating itself intelligibly to the rest of life), then we are speaking of an activity which must begin with our own faith (and lack of it) within a community of faith (and lack of it). Otherwise, we are simply studying the articulation of someone else's faith, and really doing the history of theology. The faith of which I speak here is not first of all confession, but the response of obediential hearing to the intrusive word spoken (in whatever fashion, and however encoded) by God within the project of our own lives.

Unless in some fashion I am in touch with God's intrusion into my life (and that God has so intruded is the presupposition of our coming together here), there is nothing for me to think of at all that I can call theology. If the shaping and sanctifying work of the Holy Spirit is not the essential starting point and final goal of the theological process, then I cannot but regard the 'spiritual life' as an effete form of super-erogation.

The datum of theological reflection is supplied not by tradition of God's work in the past, but by observation of God's work in the present (which observation includes the discernment of God's denial in evil). If this work is to appear anywhere, it will appear in the lives of human beings. Our theological concepts, then, should derive, not from thin air or thinner tradition, but from the careful observation of the Holy as it creates space for itself in our lives and the lives of those about us. We need to think about the hard particularity of our life: its patterns and centres, its directions and goals. These are available to our thought as we attend to the living shape of our days; we can learn to diagnose, spiritually, as surely as we can psychologically. And we begin with ourselves.

If we do not begin from such an experiential basis, our systematic and doctrinal theology, and our philosophical theology (all of which look to the clarity of the concepts and the connections, as well as to the adequacy of the tools of our thinking) will tend to float into pure abstraction. In this case, abstraction means studying someone else's way of thinking about his or her faith, rather than learning ourselves to think about our faith (and lack of it) within this community of belief (and disbelief). And this is alienation.

The concepts and creeds from the tradition are absolutely necessary, if our thinking is to be connected and coherent, but they cannot be an end in themselves. When these concepts lose their transparency to experience, they are useless. When our theological concepts no longer pertain to the experience of God's Spirit at work in the world (in our lives), they are otiose. Aquinas reminds us that the act of intellection reaches term not in the concept, but in the *reversio ad phantasma*, in the concept's enfleshment with particularity. So also in theological reflection. If my concept of grace does not derive in some fashion from my observation of how I have been gifted (without my doing and in my pain) by God, and if my concept of grace does not in turn illumine my own experience of God's presence in absence (and others' ways of waking sober and not knowing how they got there), then it can be wondered whether I have done theology at all.

But how are we to learn to think in this fashion? How can the process of learning to hear our own story, and that we share with others as the story of God's bold intrusion and iconoclasm, begin? Our experience alone, like all experience, is rooted in ambiguity, and itself needs tools of discernment. So as we attend to the grinding force of the Holy within and without us, we attend as well to the symbols of the tradition, for they speak of his work before us in the world. This means we must learn to appropriate the Old and New Testaments (the canon of scripture which is the Church's working bibliography) in a way other than as a record of activity which happened only long ago and far away.

By placing these documents of another age in a canon, that is, by making these documents the normative framework for her self-understanding (and process of self-criticism) through every age, the Church has made a clear statement. First, these writings stand as prophetic to every generation of believers, and analytic in the term prophet is the speaking of God's Word. Second, the word spoken in these writings is one which pertains immediately to life before God in every time and every place, for that is the subject matter of the scripture. They do not speak simply of a past history, but speak to a present history, and by so speaking, help create it. The subject matter of the scripture remains the same now as it was then, for God is as alive and active among human beings now as then. If this is not our presupposition, we should not read the scripture at all, and certainly not as a source for theological reflection.

We turn to the scripture, then, as eagerly and as full of anticipation as a neurotic stumbling upon a volume of Freud. In them we find (if not Life itself) the symbols by which we begin to discern and understand the Life being shaped in us by God's Spirit. It is there we learn first about the transformation of our minds by God's Spirit (Rom. 12:1–3; Col. 3:10–11), and the measure of its transformation (I Cor. 2:6–16). These texts point us to the power by which we are being reshaped (II Cor. 3:17–18), and to the freedom both given to us and set before us as goal (Gal. 5:1, 13). They also pose the question of how this power might be at work in us. What is meant, experientially, by the obedience of faith (Rom. 1:5, 16:26), and how does one learn obedience through what one suffers (Heb. 5:5–10)?

This is not a matter of proof-texting. It is a matter of reading Paul's letters to the Galatians and Colossians, for example, not simply as a record of a dispute long ago and far away about the keeping of the law and the works of asceticism, but as a testimony to Christians in every age about what constitutes maturity in Christ. Does the growth granted by the Spirit move us toward the perfectionism of the ascetical, or the availability of faith? The letters speak directly to this issue, for the issue is as fresh now as then, and it is at the heart of 'the spiritual life'.

When we read the scriptures in this way, we come to them out of the particular and fragmented questions of our individual and communal lives. We recognize that they, in turn, speak to us out of a particular, partial, and fragmented condition. Precisely the process of questioning reveals which witnesses will speak to which aspect of God's work among us. If we seek to wrap the testaments into a package (even one called 'Biblical Theology'), we silence them for our age. If we wrap our lives in a package, we stifle the question. If we are to know which questions to pose to which texts, we need to be alert first of all to the shape of our experience before God. God's work in our lives is the leading edge of an ecclesial hermeneutic.

Only if these symbols of the tradition are as alive and flexible for me as the symbols of psychology and sociology, indeed only if they are more alive and flexible for me than those, can I hope to think theologically about my (and our) experience, and therefore appropriate the 'life of the Spirit' as the heart of my theological reflection. The symbols of the scripture come first. But also the symbols shaped by the constant rereading of the scripture in the successive ages of God's working in human hearts, for these, too, are points of God's story with us of which we are the continuation. Only when these tools of discernment become flexible, supple and alive, will I find myself perceiving the person before me, marked by sin and grace, longing and suffering, as one marked by God long before I came here, marked by a God carving out a space for freedom in the world.

We cannot, therefore, talk seriously about 'spiritual formation' or 'spiritual direction' in this place until we have taken seriously the theological task of discerning how God is at work through the Holy Spirit in us and apart from us in this time.

We need at least, to learn the right questions. I think that among them are these. In what direction does growth in the Spirit go? Does it lead to the truncation of the human spirit, or its flowering? Is the route through law or freedom? If freedom, what does this mean? If not law, then what is the measure? If the measure is itself the Spirit, then do we get a clue from whose Spirit it is?

What understanding of the human person is presumed in my unreflective talk about the spiritual life? We need to ask for the anthropology involved in our theological statements. What do I say about the ability of the human spirit to transcend itself when I speak of 'grace', and when I speak so of grace, what does this imply for my understanding of incarnation? Is our being gifted by God's Spirit, so that we can, as did Jesus, call God 'Abba, my

Father,' (Rom. 8:15) simply powerful rhetoric, or does it mean something very real: that the work of the Spirit in humans leads to the replication of Jesus' movement toward the Father? And that this means through the painful self-emptying of obediential faith (Phil. 2:6ff). And that this means paying attention to the structure of life's moments, for that is where the call comes, as it did for Jesus. And this means, somehow, learning to find out about Jesus from the Gospels, and not just from historical research.

Perhaps, though, the 'spirit' of which I speak, when I talk unreflectively about the 'spiritual life' is really (even if I protest) the spirit of Platonism or Gnosticism, which seeks liberation and calm by escaping, in prayer, from the complexity and ambiguity of bodily existence. Is the goal of the spiritual life a fragile perfectionism maintained by fearful watching and defensiveness, or is it a joyful simplicity in which all that God has created is affirmed, because the gift of God's Spirit has for the first time enabled us to perceive the world fresh as new creation (II Cor. 5:17)?

Is prayer a method of centering our selfish egos in the depths of our own better 'selves,' or is it a silent, radical self-honesty before the Other who remains, not a friendly companion, but (yes, even when giving) an absence beneath our presence to ourselves? Is the prayer of silence, therefore, when the wheels of self-aggrandizement slow their spin before the Mystery which will not be seduced, only an optional bit of piety for monkish types, or is it an essential correlative to the listening which is obediential faith?

Again, about how I regard the 'Spirit'. What is my perception of my body and that of others? Do I regard the growth in the Spirit as one which moves me toward the truncation of sexuality, power, possessions and anger? Or are these aspects of being human, rooted as they are biologically, regarded by me as particularly difficult virtues to exercise? How can I be, positively, virtuous in my sexual being? How can I be angry as an act of intimacy and creative fidelity? What does my claim to my own power have to do with obedient faith? Without my own project, my own 'want', does the 'ought' of God's call have any significance at all?

9

Until we have wrestled with these questions together in an honest and reflective fashion; until we devote to these issues the same hard, concrete and creative thought we give to our lives themselves; indeed, until these questions become the questions by which we attend to our lives, we have no business speaking of spiritual life or spiritual formation, for we have, literally, not given the first thought to it.

Maybe that is why we have not spoken of it more, together. Or is it because we regard the whole business as insignificant, trivial, fit for lesser minds? That itself would be revealing. Perhaps, on the other hand, we might be a bit daunted by the way in which our thought must in these matters remain flexible and alive, must resist reduction to lecture notes, must be in constant contact with life experience (that we live and that lived by others). Perhaps we are a bit threatened by the way this particular subject has a nasty way of turning from being a subject questioned to a subject which questions.

Maybe, in the long run, we have simply not given much thought to what we might mean when we speak of theology not as a way of studying someone else's thought, but precisely as a way of thinking about reality, our own reality. I think it is time for us to start thinking about the spiritual life as the Life of God's Spirit. I suggest we need to have precisely that issue at the heart of all our theological enterprise. This will involve our own faith in ways we cannot predict, and in ways which will certainly be frightening. But it is, I think, the only way we really begin to become theologians, and not just academicians. I am suggesting something, that is, not about the direction of our curriculum, but about the direction of our hearts and heads.

Chapter 2

Suffering, Sin and Scripture

Suffering is hard to think about, speak about, or write about. But most of all it is hard to do. Those who are in pain – most of the world's population at any given moment – do not do a lot of thinking, speaking or writing about suffering. All their energy goes into surviving. That is why a lot of what is said and written about suffering seems hollow to those actually in pain. They see an unbridgeable gap between those able to think or speak or write, and those (like them) who can only manage to survive by gritting their teeth.

Once when I was young and (more) stupid I tried reading the Book of Job to my wife when she was in serious pain. I discovered quickly that words of great nobility cannot even be heard by one whose body is being tortured. I learned eventually that simple silence and the holding of her hand were better than any eloquence, even that of the Bible.

It is nevertheless important that those of us sufficiently free from pain at the moment to think at all should think hard and well about suffering, for it falls into one of those fundamental categories which, when we get wrong, we also *go* wrong. And I think there is a lot of bad thinking in our world today about suffering, which actually adds to people's pain.

I have in mind primarily the contemporary heresy that more or less identifies suffering and evil. This is a dreadful error, first of all because it makes evil a cosmological rather than a moral category, with the unintended consequence that suffering is trivialized and evil is made banal. It also deprives suffering of any positive value. A reality that is actually deeply ambiguous and polyvalent is reduced to something simply negative and is thereby distorted.

SUFFERING DEFINED

The easy equation between suffering and evil results in part, I think, from a failure adequately to formulate what we actually mean by suffering. For something so central to our human experience, the term remains strangely undefined, enabling casual conceptual connections and slippery logic. Let me propose that we begin our thinking with clarity. Let us think of suffering as the pain of a system in disequilibrium. It is obvious from the start that the use of 'pain' means that suffering is restricted to sentient systems. A mechanical system can fall into disequilibrium, but it cannot be said to suffer, for it is not sentient.

To feel pain, then, requires life. But to be alive means also always to be in disequilibrium, for change is the single constant of mortal life. Therefore all living things suffer as a consequence of existence. The higher the level of sentience and the more complex the form of life (with all its simultaneous changes) the greater the potential for suffering. We guess that plants suffer. We can vividly imagine the suffering of animals. But we know human suffering, for it is ours.

Human suffering happens at the physical level when an organic system is diseased or injured or dying. It happens at the psychological level when a soul is tortured or traumatized by emotion. It happens at the mental level when cognitive dissonance is experienced.

When pain is inflicted on another in order to make the organism sick or damaged, or in order to bruise another's heart, or in order to confuse another's mind, then it is legitimate and even necessary to speak of evil. To cause needless suffering is to do evil. But the evil resides in the intent to do harm, not in the suffering itself, which is a natural function of all living beings.

It is critical to observe, however, that systems also fall into disequilibrium – and therefore experience pain – from positive causes. Bodies that grow in size experience pain – ask gangly adolescents or serious bodybuilders – and bodies that give birth experience enormous pain. The cost of physical life itself is suffering. Likewise, a soul that grows in compassion does so through pain. And all learning involves pain, a truth so obvious the ancient Greeks coined the motto, *mathein pathein*, 'to learn is to suffer'; a contemporary rendering is the one used by athletes, 'no pain, no gain'.

The pain in such cases is no less real, the suffering no less significant. How then is it different? Because it is pain that leads to the increase of life rather than its decrease.

It is our contemporary culture's tragedy to have lost any sense of suffering as a positive dimension of human existence. Beginning with the premise that life ought to be without pain, we make suffering something to be avoided at all cost. We consider the equation between evil and suffering so self-evident that we make avoiding suffering the equal of fighting evil. No wonder we are the most narcotized generation ever to inhabit the earth, searching for ever more effective addictive patterns to anaesthetize our existence. No wonder that despite centuries of tradition that has taken the cross of Jesus to be the sign of God's loving presence, ours is the first generation in which those calling themselves Christian theologians question whether the cross is a viable symbol, since it seems to justify the suffering of the oppressed.

DIMENSION OF LIFE

In light of our deep confusion on this issue, it is all the more important to remember the grounds of our Christian self-understanding. In the mystery of God's self-revelation in Jesus Christ our Lord, it is in how Jesus' death and resurrection reveals to us God's own inner life that we learn how suffering is a dimension of life that we cannot and should not avoid or expunge.

It is a dimension which, through the gift of God's own life, we might transfigure.

The difference between the Old Testament and the New Testament in their respective views of human suffering is fundamental. For the most part, the Old Testament's view is close to that of contemporary culture.

The Old Testament views human suffering in completely negative terms. Suffering is a sign that something is wrong. The ideal world should be one without suffering, where childbirth is without pain and where bread can be obtained without the sweat of the brow. If it were not for sin, the Edenic myth has it, things would be so.

Since Torah teaches that God blesses the righteous with long life, progeny, prosperity and security, it follows that poverty, barrenness, illness, instability and an early death are forms of God's curse. Righteousness should mean freedom from suffering, unrighteousness should demand suffering. This deuteronomistic principle is driven home repeatedly in the histories of the people. Over and over the lesson for individuals and the nation is asserted in the biblical narratives: when people are righteous, then God blesses them; when they suffer, it is because they have broken covenant with God.

A NEW EXPERIENCE OF GOD

Each in its own way, the books associated with Qoheleth and Job challenge this premise. The Preacher's scepticism questions a necessary connection between righteousness and human suffering, and Job's righteous sufferer fights for a hearing against those whose pious prating insists that his suffering results from his sin. But neither Qoheleth nor Job is able to break decisively with the basic understanding of suffering as misfortune. The same is true of those other voices of the suffering in the texts of the Old Testament: the psalmist, oppressed by the wicked, cries for vindication from God and liberation from his suffering; even the mysterious servant of Isaiah whose silent suffering will later be used to illuminate the meaning of Jesus' death for others gives only oblique and obscure promise of a fuller revelation of God's capacity to enter into human freedom.

It is important to note that the New Testament's perspective on suffering – and therefore also our perspective – is not shaped by an infusion of a new philosophy, but by a new experience of God in Jesus Christ that enabled human thought to reach a point it had not before. Three aspects of this deserve emphasis. First, we see in Jesus' ministry and, above all, in his death and resurrection, a mode of suffering that is life-giving. Second, in Jesus and the sending of the Holy Spirit we see the self-revelation of God's own inner life. Third, what we have learned of God in Jesus enables us to think about human suffering in terms of creation rather than simply in terms of destruction.

COMPASSION

In the Gospels, the characteristic of Jesus that is perhaps most compelling – especially because of its unexpectedness in the world of antiquity – is his compassion. He is the one who 'suffers with' others. Although he teaches, he is not merely a sage who discourses on the social and political systems of the day. Although he touches the outcast, he is not simply a thaumaturge who with a word or a wink can heal all ills. Jesus is not a revealer of divine truths who floats serenely above ordinary human experience. He is, as the Letter to the Hebrews says, 'like his brethren in every respect . . . because he himself has suffered and been tempted, he is able to help those who are tempted' (Heb. 2:17–18). Time and again, the Gospels show Jesus feeling the pain felt by others, whether in the struggles over his messianic identity, or in confronting the helpless poor and outcast and ill, or in the agony of facing a death he did not desire. He not only experiences what all other humans experience of pain and loss and grief, he reaches out to the pain of others and participates in it. It is when Jesus sees the crowd like sheep without a shepherd that he is 'moved with compassion' (Mark 6:34). It is when he hears of his friend's death

15

that Jesus weeps (John 11:35). It is when Jesus sees his listeners hungry that he seeks to provide them with food out of his own resources (Matt. 14:16).

The Jesus of the Gospels is instantly recognizable among all the saints of scripture and all the heroes of antiquity as uniquely the one who suffered with and for others so that they might be empowered with more life. Jesus is defined in terms of a radical faith and obedience towards God that is spelled out in radical self-disposing service and love for others. His final meal with his followers at which he broke the bread and gave it to them as his body and poured out the wine and asked them to drink it as his blood was therefore absolutely consistent with his ministry of presence to the poor and in direct continuity with the body language of self-dispossession expressed by the feeding of the multitude on the mountain. Jesus' suffering of death on the cross therefore was the final and logical expression of a life so defined, an obedience to God so profound it can only be called *kenosis*, a self-emptying, and a gift of service to others so absolute that it must be termed the act of a *doulos*, a slave (see Phil. 2:5–11).

The entire ground of Christian existence is the conviction – based in real human experience – that this suffering and death of Jesus led to the most powerful and pervasive outpouring of God's life on humanity through the gift of the Holy Spirit, because Jesus' resurrection from the dead was an entry into the very life of God, an empowerment that made him 'life-giving Spirit' (1 Cor. 15:45). Here is the existential basis for reversing the common perception of suffering: our experience of new and more powerful life through the suffering and death of Jesus Christ our Lord. And it is this realization that in Jesus we have to do not only with a good man of the past but a powerful presence of God in the present, that forces us to consider how what we have seen in the humanity of Jesus is a fundamental revelation of God's own life that can also reshape our lives.

SHARED LIFE OF PAIN

This consideration is the doctrine of the incarnation: that in Jesus, God entered fully into the fabric of human existence, and shared fully the pain of human life. In the suffering saviour Jesus we have seen revealed the suffering face of God, who has reached across that infinite distance between the creator and creation in an all-encompassing embrace, who has taken up in God's own life the suffering of all humanity through the one whom we have learned to call God's Son. Paul says that 'God was in Christ reconciling the world to himself' (2 Cor. 5:19). All the tomes of Christian theology have not adequately exhausted the significance of that simple declaration which so perfectly expresses the central Christian conviction concerning Jesus. In learning Jesus, we learn God.

What we learn of God through Jesus is a glimpse of a living community within God, a community of giving and receiving between persons in such fashion that life increases rather than decreases with the giving and receiving and giving back again. We catch sight of a life within God that can grow by encompassing God's own creation. We can even suspect that the trinitarian God that shows us such glimpses of his inner life through the veiled revelation in creation, salvation, and sanctification, may be the supreme system in disequilibrium, the ultimate expression of the truth that suffering change is the price paid for life to grow. To say such things is to skirt the edges of orthodoxy, yet our experience of Jesus and the gift of God's Spirit gives us boldness.

Such truths are difficult, perhaps even dangerous, to speak; how can we speak of the changeless, immortal, impassible, perfect God as revealing to us suffering at the heart of God's own life? We draw away from such flat assertions because they so fundamentally conflict with the sorts of beliefs about God that declare God to be unchangeable, impassible, immortal and perfect. Yet our experience of God in Christ tugs our thought, pulls it temptingly towards this dizzying vision. Is it perhaps that God seems changeless to us mainly because the way God changes is so profound and all-encompassing that our categories are altogether outstripped?

But if we cannot find the right words to state this truth about God, we can find ways to live this truth, which is both simple and difficult. We seek to live even as God has shown us God's own life in Christ. We therefore do not avoid suffering as an evil, we do not narcotize ourselves against pain, we do not seek to hold our lives securely as a system in perfect balance. Rather, we recognize that stress and suffering are not only intrinsic to all life, they are entries into the deepest mystery of life itself. In the name and in the power of Jesus, we therefore embrace the suffering that comes to us as the opportunity for transfiguration, as the path towards transformation into that self-emptying giving and being filled again ever more richly that is God's own life.

Chapter 3

Wealth and Property in the New Testament

What are the attitudes to wealth and property in the New Testament? The best place to start with this topic is to recognize its difficulty. It's not that the New Testament lacks such attitudes or even an abundance of prescriptions concerning wealth and property. The problem is rather that the NT seems to address a world very different from our own and it seems to prescribe mutually irreconcilable things. At one point, we are told to give up all our possessions; at another, to give alms or to pool all our possessions in common, or to work with our hands to support ourselves or to be supported by the community for the work we do for the community.

If our interest in the New Testament were primarily antiquarian, such variety would be merely a pleasant puzzle. But when we seek guidance for our lives in the NT, the diversity of its prescriptions is confusing. On the question of possessions, as on so many other points of vital interest, the answer to the question, 'What does the New Testament teach on X?' is usually, 'Which NT book have you last read?' Those who claim to live in exact accord with the prescriptions of the New Testament are lying either to others or themselves, for the diversity in the New Testament makes such adherence impossible. All of us must make some sort of selection among its prescriptions.

In this chapter, I bracket questions concerning the normative use of the New Testament. Bracketing of the normative question does not mean I think it irrelevant. Just the opposite: it is so important that it should not be carried out casually or uncritically. Nor will I go into the equally important question of why the New Testament contains such a variety of prescriptions, although when we remember the circumstances under which the New Testament was written the most astonishing thing about it is not its lack of consistency but rather that it has any coherence at all. These writings were not composed in circumstances of leisure and reflection. They were written during a time of rapid expansion, radical adjustment, and severe duress. The writers were interested above all in understanding their experience of the transforming power of God as it came to them from the unlikely source of a crucified Messiah. Their attempts at connecting this experience to consistent patterns of behaviour were necessarily inchoate and haphazard.

The literary and thematic diversity of the New Testament is only one of the hurdles in reflecting on the connection between authentic Christian existence and the uses of wealth and property. Another is the apparent gulf between the world addressed by the New Testament and the present world. How can any of its directives be relevant to a world whose economy is global in character, corporate in structure and systemically interdependent?

RECENT RESEARCH

One of the greatest contributions of recent research into earliest Christianity, however, has been to challenge the assumption of infinite distance between the circumstances of the first Christians and ourselves. The last few decades have seen the increased use of social scientific methods in the study of antiquity. Such methods have enabled us to test theoretical models for the development of early Christianity. More importantly, they have alerted historians who had tended to be more interested in ideas than in things to the specifically social dimensions of life within which ideas were formed. One result has been a fuller and more highly nuanced picture of the world in which Christianity was born and the New Testament birthed. Another has been the need to adjust some of our traditional perceptions concerning the early Christians.

EMPIRE

What are we learning? First, we have become increasingly aware of the overall social and economic complexity of the Graeco-Roman world. Earlier analysis saw this world in highly simple terms: there were extremes of poverty and wealth, with wealth being in the hands of the aristocratic few and grinding poverty being the lot of the oppressed majority. Now, there is no question that the fact of empire had real consequences for macro-economics. Empire sponsored the plundering of territories and the importation of their treasures to the city in extravagant triumphal processions; the transportation of slaves to various parts of the empire; the foundation of military colonies throughout new conquests to secure stability but also to establish markets; the harnessing of mining and engineering for instruments of war; the excessive taxation levied on troublesome provinces; the worrisome necessity of ensuring regular shipments of grain from Alexandria so that the urban proletariat in the city might not grow restless and rebellious – Claudius guaranteed double pay for ships daring to make the Mediterranean crossing during the dangerous months between October and May.

The world of empire was one of great social stratification with extremes of wealth and poverty, but it would be a mistake to locate everyone at the extremes or to think of the economy as a static or completely state-driven system. The term 'middle class' may be anachronistic when applied to antiquity, but not distortingly so: between the extremes represented by the great absentee land-owners on the one hand, who spent their working time at the city and their leisure time at the country villa, and the day labourers who could not guarantee food from one day to the next, were countless people who had and produced goods and wealth, if often of modest proportions. Both slaves and free persons were merchants and craftspeople and traders and even entrepreneurs, who by dint of their effort and brains could climb, if not to the aristocracy, at least to the envied ranks of the *nouveau riche*.

In the *Satyricon*, Petronius sketches the fabulous career of a certain Trimalchio. He began as a slave who managed his master's property. Freed at the master's death, he was also his heir. But rather than sit on his inherited property, he sold it all for capital, and began a career as an entrepreneur. He built ships and carried out trade. He lost five ships and 30 million sesterces in a single storm – remember the danger of the Mediterranean in winter months – but built another fleet and made still more money. He then stopped trading and became a financier, sponsoring other traders. Finally he accumulated a fortune so vast as to allow him to purchase great stretches of property in Italy and Sicily. Trimalchio was exceptional in his meteoric rise, but not unique. The NT itself everywhere paints the picture of a highly mobile, commercially engaged class of people, whose travels across the Mediterranean were driven by the profit motive, and who also brought with them in their travels messages about strange gods and new beliefs. Such were the craftspeople Aquila and Priscilla whom Paul met in Corinth shortly after they had been expelled from Rome; such were the members of the urban dog and pony prophecy show Paul met on the streets of Philippi; in another way, such was the guild of silversmiths servicing the great temple of Artemis in Ephesus and all her tributary shrines throughout Asia Minor.

FIRST BELIEVERS

This leads to a second observation about the social world of early Christianity: the first believers not only met such folk, they were among them. For a long time, it was supposed that Christianity was made up primarily of the oppressed classes, the slaves and outcasts who had no hope for a human future and so were particularly predisposed to an other-worldly message of salvation and a this-worldly offer of a community of possessions. Jesus was himself a poor man and called the poor to follow him, and Christianity, in Marxist terms, was regarded as a sort of proletarian movement whose social marginalization and resentment led to the construction of a utopian counterculture.

Two kinds of consideration have led scholars to modify that perception. First, we have learned more about the social functions of language itself: people who call themselves the poor and who attack outsiders as wealthy may be using property language in a symbolic rather than a literal way. Such communities may be marginalized in any number of ways – in terms of status, intellectual respectability, honour – but these do not necessarily include economic deprivation. Second, more careful attention to the specific facts about wealth in the empire and the diversity of classes within that society enables us better to situate the Christian movement in economic terms.

The results are startling. When we look at Jesus and his followers in Galilee, we don't see day labourers with no money for the following day. Jesus was *tektōn*, a craftsman in wood who might have found work in Sepphoris, a Hellenistic city within easy walking distance of Nazareth. Peter, James and John were not impoverished fishermen but small-time entrepreneurs with several boats and hired hands, suppliers of Galilean fish-markets. Paul's communities did not have the truly powerful and wealthy among them, but they had some people whose means were considerably larger than others. Householders like Stephanus and Achaicus served as financial patrons of the church in Corinth. Phoebe was also a financial patron of Paul in Cenchrae and his business agent to the church at Rome. Chloe was a female householder whose servants delivered news of crisis at Corinth to Paul. Property-owning women like Lydia or Nympha made their houses available to the community for worship. Slave-owners like Philemon provided generous assistance to the Pauline churches. The facts presupposed by the literature of the New Testament suggest a movement whose economic and social location is at neither extreme of power and wealth but rather in a flexible middle that could include a fair range of disparity in wealth and property.

STATUS SEEKING

This brings us to a third point, the way in which from the beginning such disparities created difficulties within the Christian movement. Once more, the stereotype of insiders all being poor and persecuted while outsiders were all wealthy oppressors is simplistic. Social tensions existed within the community because of differences in gender, race, and social location, the classic markers of status. Tensions were generated as well by disparities in wealth. Indeed, some of the language about rich and poor in the New Testament – for example in the gospel of Luke and the letter of James – has the precise purpose of challenging insiders who had greater material possessions to also have appropriate social attitudes.

The Corinthian correspondence is a particularly good source of information. When Paul responds to reports of troubles at the Lord's supper – some are apparently stuffing themselves and some are going hungry – we are able to understand the problem better because of our awareness of the customs concerning patronage in the Graeco-Roman world. Public banquets were financed by wealthy patrons. The payoff for such benefaction was sitting at the head table with one's friends and eating first and best, while those who depended on others ate last and worst. This was the way of the world. Obviously some Corinthians thought this way of arranging things should apply in the Church as well. Paul thought otherwise. Likewise James castigates those who in their assembly give deference to a richly dressed person while showing disrespect to someone wearing rags. Such situations suggest that dealing with the wealthy was a fundamental problem for the early Christians. On the one hand they were needed for hospitality, support for the mission, care for the poor. On the other hand, their culturally conditioned assumption that authority should accompany benefaction was resisted. Indeed, they were subjected to unremitting criticism of wealth and its capacity to smother faith.

MONEY TROUBLES

We can see how the issue of money clouded Paul's relationships with the Corinthian church. There was first the question of his own support. He had made it a matter of principle not to accept money for his preaching to that church, even though, he insisted, he had the right to be supported. But he was somewhat disingenuous, for he did not reveal to the Corinthians that he was being supported financially by the Philippian church during the time of his Corinthian ministry. But real trouble did not start until Paul decided to carry out his great fund-raising venture for the Jerusalem church. He wanted to symbolize unity between Jews and Gentiles by bringing to the Jewish mother community in Jerusalem a great collection of money from Gentile churches he had founded. So after leaving Corinth he sends his delegate to ask the Corinthians to kick in large amounts of money for this grand gesture of reconciliation. Not surprisingly, the Corinthians are shocked. They think Paul is being dishonest, and accuse him and his delegate Titus of fraud. No wonder that they prefer other preachers who asked for an honest dollar up front for an honest day's preaching, rather than this 'send the cheque later' routine from Paul. It does Paul little good to smear his rivals as 'peddlers of God's word' for the Corinthians consider him to be something even worse.

It does not take a great deal of imagination to draw analogies between these tensions of early Christianity and our own lives. We too live in a highly mobile, highly commercial world that is interlinked and interdependent in ways astonishingly similar to the ancient imperial world. We too find it necessary as we live in this world to juggle our religious commitments with the pressing and sometimes incompatible demands of business. We recognize in the Corinthian church patterns remarkably familiar to some of our own. We know all too well the uneasy role of the wealthy patron in the parish, whose benefactions are eagerly sought yet also resented, whose status in the world and service in the Church are not easily aligned. We recognize the deep ambiguities in issues of support for the clergy and fundraising for the Church, and how (spectacularly in the case of televangelists, subtly in the case of Father Jones) issues of financial management create spiritual crises and rivalries as real and dangerous as those experienced by Paul.

In short, we have come to know much more about the world of the New Testament, the social and economic status of the first Christians, and the problems involving wealth and property within the Christian movement from the beginning. Such knowledge is not irrelevant to the way we set about applying the New Testament to our lives. By making that world addressed by the texts more like our own, we can better understand the purpose and perspective of the diverse NT prescriptions. This does not mean that translation to our own lives is either automatic or easy, but it will be more responsible and informed as we try to sort out how those statements speak to our own lives.

Chapter 4

Sacrifice is the Body Language of Love

Like sin and suffering, sacrifice has for many these days become a problematic part of the Christian theological lexicon. I recently met two women who had some advanced theological education at a production of *The Elephant Man*. I told them that I was thinking about the topic of sacrifice. Their reaction was typical: what, they said, could I possibly find to say about a subject that no one with any sophistication any longer took seriously? So I asked them what immediately came to mind when they heard the word 'sacrifice'. One replied, the slaughter of helpless animals; the other said, the oppression of women. Clearly, this is a term in need of some rehabilitation.

In fact, sacrifice has had an uneasy place within Christianity from the beginning. We remember that Jesus continued the prophetic criticism of ritual sacrifices offered in place of social justice. Quoting Joel, he twice declared in Matthew's gospel, 'Go learn what this means: I desire mercy and not sacrifice, says the Lord' (Matt. 9:13; 12:7). And the Letter to the Hebrews definitively distances the new covenant from that which was expressed 'in the blood of goats and calves' (Heb. 9:12). Together with circumcision and the rest of the ritual observance of Torah, the new dispensation repudiated animal sacrifices, considering all the elaborate language prescribing sacrifices only a 'shadow of the good things to come' in Christ (Heb. 10:1).

And it is to Christ that sacrifice language attaches in the New Testament. The same Paul who rejects circumcision for Gentile believers says of Jesus, 'Christ our Passover has been sacrificed' (I Cor. 5:7). The same author of Hebrews who considers animal sacrifices obsolescent says that Christ 'removes sin by the sacrifice of himself' (Heb. 9:27). And the Jesus who says that God prefers mercy to sacrifice describes his own symbolic sharing of himself at his last meal with words that echo the sacrificial act that sealed the Mosaic covenant: the cup is 'new covenant in my blood' (Luke 22:20).

EXPIATION AND OBEDIENCE

Paul likewise speaks of Jesus' death in terms of the blood that was sprinkled on the 'mercy seat' on the Day of Atonement (Rom. 3:25). John writes in his first letter that Jesus makes 'expiation through his blood' (1 John 1:7) and Peter likewise speaks of Jesus' death in terms of a sacrificial 'sprinkling of blood' (1 Pet. 1:19). The dramatic shift accomplished by the New Testament is from external to internal, from the offering of things to the offering of the self, and these shifts find their focus in Jesus' obedience unto death.

It is because Jesus, in turn, is considered both the source of salvation and the measure of discipleship, that sacrifice lives on in Christian consciousness. The dual appreciation is expressed perfectly by the eucharistic liturgy. The symbolic sharing of bread and wine in memory of Jesus takes on the specific language of sacrifice. It remains, for many older Christians, the 'Holy Sacrifice of the Mass', the supreme means by which the grace won by Jesus' obedient death reaches the hearts of believers. At the same time, his gesture of sharing himself through his death and resurrection becomes the pattern for Christians to imitate: 'Do this in memory of me.'

All of this seems an appropriate, even necessary, development out of the New Testament's ambivalent attitude toward sacrifice. How, then, did we reach the state of mind that finds the very mention of sacrifice repulsive? How could we get to the point where a Womanist theologian can declare that the cross is no longer a viable symbol for Christians – or at least not for Christian women of colour – because it has become less an instrument of liberation than an instrument of oppression? If you, like me, find this reaction extreme, it is nevertheless important for us to recognize that it is only the brave and explicit articulation of a mood that is far more prevalent among contemporary believers, who find any use of sacrifice language to be offensive.

WRATHFUL GOD?

Christian theologians and preachers are themselves responsible for much of the distortion. Theologians got into heated and highly technical debates over the doctrine of atonement, in which the role of Christ's sacrifice frequently played a key role. When a theory of atonement portrays the death of Jesus as a 'necessary' sacrifice in order to appease a wrathful God or to pay off a debt incurred to Satan, a positive view of sacrifice, or of God, is difficult to maintain. When disputes breaking out over the 'sacrificial' character of the Eucharist led to language being used about the bread and wine that so emphasized the 'renewal' of Christ's death that crass physicalism replaced delicate symbolism, the use of sacrificial language itself can easily seem the culprit.

Preachers have been much worse. They have found it all too easy to demand sacrifice of others, above all women. Women have been exhorted to 'sacrifice their children' to the priesthood and religious life, to 'sacrifice themselves' to the needs of their husbands and children, even when these 'needs' sometimes expressed themselves in abusive and even violent forms. Similarly, people have been asked to 'sacrifice' their possessions for the support of the Church and its projects. In some traditions, indeed, the main focus of sacrifice is found in the demand of financial tithing. The rhetoric of sacrifice, in other words, has often become a rhetoric by which the weak and powerless are manipulated. The internalization of this rhetoric, in turn, has contributed significantly to the perception of Christianity, even by many of its adherents, as joyless and life-denying. There are two elements of distortion in this language of sacrifice. The first is that it emphasizes cost rather than gain, the loss of life more than the enhancement of life. The second is that it imposes sacrifice as a necessary form of suffering more than it evokes self-giving as a free expression of love.

SELF-FULFILMENT

It must also be admitted, however, that another factor enters into the decline of sacrifice language in present-day Christianity. Ours is an age that has a strong bias in favour of self-fulfilment and personal empowerment, partly in response to the perception that traditional religion has served to suppress legitimate self-development and expression. In the name of 'self-identity' and 'personal integrity' some Christians surround themselves with walls of defence against anyone else taking advantage of them. They think of marriage in terms of a contract with all obligations divided fifty-fifty, rather than in terms of an open-ended covenant. They fit child-rearing (often through surrogates) into the trajectories of their careers. They are perfectly at home in the individualism, consumerism, and commodification that characterize modern capitalist society. So pronounced are these tendencies among some contemporary Christians that their attitudes are hard to distinguish from old-fashioned selfishness, even when they are clothed in forms of 'spirituality' that make self-centring and tranquillity absolute good. For such Christians, no rhetoric concerning sacrifice can be heard positively.

Christians' state of alienation from their own language – above all the language of Scripture, which remains the irreplaceable font of all other Christian language – is a cause for the greatest concern. This is not a matter simply of finding the words of scripture strange because we do not understand their historical context. Little labour or thought is required to learn the basics: that 'sacrifice' derives from *sacrum facere* ('to make holy') and is used to translate a variety of Hebrew and Greek expressions denoting the dedication of gifts to God, in the Old Testament including everything from thank-offerings to sin-offerings. It is rather a matter of finding them strange because we can find in our own lives no reality or truth corresponding to them. The 'relevance' of Scripture increasingly is reduced to the parts we find meaningful rather than those parts that challenge us more fundamentally, perhaps by making us ask why we find some things meaningful and others not. The way to recovering an honest engagement with Scripture's challenge is therefore not through formal anthropological analyses of sacrifice, but through reflection on ordinary human experience, and on our own personal experience.

EXPRESSES THE TRUTH OF EXISTENCE

The religious act called sacrifice makes sense if it expresses the truth of actual human existence. The truth expressed by sacrifice is that humans are profoundly dependent creatures whose life is most enhanced when it is shared, even at great cost. The question for us is whether that is also our truth, or whether we construct our lives in ways to suppress or deny that truth.

The truth is expressed through a story fairly common in the United States today. A young and talented African-American athlete receives a huge bonus for signing with a professional sports franchise. He is now worth tens of millions of dollars. His characteristic first action? Buying his mother a house. What is significant is not the amount spent, but the meaning of the act. Many of these young men were raised in poverty by only one parent, most often their mother. To enable their sons to realize their talents, these mothers worked day and night. At the same time, the young men spent countless hours practising their sport, developing their skills, so that not only they could escape poverty but also all of their family as well. Giving his mother a house is an act of love and gratitude. It expresses the athlete's recognition that his life could not have flourished had his mother not given so generously from her own life. She had not sought pleasure and possessions apart from her children, but worked selflessly so that they might have better lives.

31

MADE HOLY

The athlete's 'sacrifice' of his first salary is a purely spontaneous expression of common life: 'Mom, as you have given everything to me, I want to give something to you.' It is not a payback, it is not commensurate. How could any amount of money repay all those years of toil and want? Yet the gift given for gift received elevates both mother and child. In the exchange, both are made holy. In this common example, we see that sacrifice is a species of gift-giving motivated by love, not to the diminishment but to the enhancement of life through the sharing of it.

Sacrifice can similarly be learned from the observation of persons whose marriage genuinely symbolizes a relationship of love. Within such interpersonal love, sacrifice is a constant dimension of mutual gift-giving. To love truly, indeed, means to seek the flourishing of the other's life, which very often demands the curbing of my own desires. Gift-giving here means much more than the exchange of material things. It means the extraordinarily complex negotiations of common life that create a culture of mutual exchange and consideration so thick that even anthropologists could never disentangle its subtle nuances. Even in the delicate dance of erotic pleasure, husband and wife enter a sphere of larger joy through seeking less their own than the other's true and deep pleasure. The same is true of the daily round of life together; it is possible at all only because each seeks the other's interest even more than one's own. And this means an often painful sense of loss. But paradoxically, what appears as a form of death reveals itself as a larger life. Making room for the other in my life means the enlargement of my heart. Such gift-giving 'makes holy' the shared life that is greater and richer in being through the willingness of each to seek what is good for the other rather than the self. Genuine married love can never adequately be limned through a contract that spells out reciprocal obligations. It must be an open-ended covenant in which each partner is willing to give everything in self-disregarding and spontaneous generosity.

FOOLISHNESS OF GENEROSITY

The painful wisdom learned through the foolishness of generosity and hospitality that couples learn through their covenant with each other prepares them in part – never entirely! – for the even greater foolishness of having and raising children. We all know that parents do not make children but that children make parents. They force themselves into our lives and displace all our comfortable routines. In order to give them life and nourishment we must have less and less that we call our own. Often we end up without even a spot on the couch we can call our own.

Authentic parenting is one long sacrificial act that does not end even when children grow up and move away. Even more than in the marriage relationship, parenting reveals the way that sacrifice at once diminishes our life as we knew it ('Where is my favourite sweater? Who took my toast? The dog did *what*?') while at the same time revealing to us larger and infinitely more fascinating forms of life ('Tiffany took her first steps. Kim got married. Joby made a recording'), that are not other than our own life but an enlarged expression of our own life. Parents know experientially that the very process which makes them suffer also makes them grow. What they give never comes back in the same form. But what they are given in return is a share in a depth of being created by the gifts of knowledge, love and care, that they have given, moment by moment, in the hurly-burly of family turmoil. As in the case of marriage, there is no blueprint, no contract, for this body language of love. As in marriage, the arts of sacrifice are learned from each other through complex and delicate manœuvres of generosity.

BODY LANGUAGE

Paying close attention to human experience can help us recover some sense of the meaning of sacrifice as the body language of love. We do not thereby automatically possess a key to all the complex scriptural language concerning sacrifice. Indeed, even scholars who devote their lives to the decipherment of such things still find these difficult puzzles to solve. But we may be closer to appreciating the deep humanity that is involved even in ancient animal sacrifices. People who offer to God a first-portion of the grain of their field or the grapes of their vines thereby recognize that God gave the life that comes from the consumption of bread and wine. People who likewise offer the first lamb or goat of the flock thereby recognize the gift of life that God gives through these animals. Gratitude and love for the Creator are expressed by the donation of a portion of the Creator's gifts on the altar and in the flame. To give up a small portion of that life is to acknowledge that all of life is a gift that must be reciprocated.

RETURN FOR GIFTS

It is not at all a matter, as some anthropologists have suggested, of 'giving in order to get', as though God were being manipulated. Just the opposite: sacrifice is a gift in return for gifts given. In our world, we harvest far more crops and slaughter far more animals every year than people did in biblical times. Yet animals today are slaughtered mechanically and apart from any human meaning except that of consumption and financial profit. Are we then really morally superior to those who donated a part of their livelihood in gratitude to the One who gave them all life? The prophetic condemnation of sacrifice, remember, was not a con-demnation of the spirit of gratitude and love towards the Creator, but a condemnation of ritual that was unaccompanied by the body language of love towards the neighbour.

And it is precisely as body language of love towards the neigh-bour that we best understand the sacrifice of Jesus. The Letter to the Hebrews does speak of Jesus' faithful death in terms of the sacrifice of the day of atonement which was offered to effect and express reconciliation between God and humans. This is why, for Hebrews, Jesus needed to be both human and divine, so that in his very person he might effect such 'mediation' in an act of priesthood that was the offering of his own self: 'And it is by God's will that we have been sanctified through the offering of the body of Jesus Christ once for all' (Heb. 10:10). The main emphasis of the New Testament, however, is on Jesus' self-donation for the sake of others. 'The Son of Man', Jesus declares in Mark 10:45, 'came not to be served but to serve, and to give his life as a ransom for many.' He gives his life, in other words, so that others might be liberated. His gift of life is to enhance the life of others. John's Gospel speaks of Jesus as the Good Shepherd who 'lays down his life for the sheep' (10:15) so that 'they might have life and have it abundantly' (10:10). John expresses the logic of sacrifice this way: 'unless a grain of wheat falls into the earth and dies, it remains just a single grain: but if it dies, then it bears much fruit' (John 12:24). At his last meal, according to Luke 22:19, Jesus told his followers while breaking bread: 'This is my body, which is given for you.' The ritual gesture points backward to Jesus' entire ministry 'for the sake of many', and forward to his death. This is why Paul speaks of Jesus as the one 'who loved me and gave himself for me' (Gal. 2:20). Because Jesus is at once the 'yes' of God to humans in fidelity and also humanity's 'yes' to God in faith, we are lifted into a higher life than we could ever imagine, a sharing in the life – and the eternal dance of gifts given and received – of the triune God.

In truth, we do not know why God has gifted us with life through the death of Jesus. We have no special access to the divine blueprint for salvation. What we have is the gift, and that is enough. From the gift, we learn in turn how to live according to the 'mind of Christ' (1 Cor. 2:16) in seeking others' interests even more than our own (Phil. 2:1–11), learn how to be led by the Spirit to 'bear one another's burdens' and so 'fulfil the pattern of the Christ' (Gal. 6:2). And from the gift we might also be allowed to think that our God loves wildly, foolishly, splendidly, and super-abundantly, is willing to risk God's own life so that the life of creatures might flourish, is willing to empty out completely so as to fill all things with glory.

Chapter 5

Preaching the Resurrection

Christianity has certainly gone through its share of puzzling and at times perverse permutations, even as it surprised the world first by its unlikely success, then by its astonishing creativity, and now by its rude insistence on survival long after all the best minds have declared it wrong, irrelevant, and, when not silly, downright harmful.

Perhaps none of its changes has been so profound as the one which made 'the resurrection' one topic among many to which one might devote preaching, rather than the single, all-encompassing reality out of which and concerning which the act of preaching is empowered. And no gap is more worth leaping than that separating those of us who think about the resurrection of Jesus as something that happened to him rather than to us, and as something hard to make seem real, and the first Christians, whose convictions concerning the resurrection started with what happened to them, and first defied, then defined their thinking about all reality. What is at stake is at least understanding what the New Testament is talking about, and, by the way, the very nature of Christian faith.

Leaping across that gap in consciousness, however, is difficult and requires some imagination. We can start by recognizing the divergent starting places for our evaluation of Jesus. At the beginning of the Christian movement, what distinguished insiders and outsiders was whether they saw Jesus' significance ending or beginning with his death. For those who – like Paul in his early career – measured Jesus 'according to the flesh', Jesus' claims to be messiah had to be established entirely within the frame of his earthly ministry. This meant for most Jews, and for many Gentile critics, that Jesus was demonstrably a false messiah or failed philosopher, for his death was 'foolishness to the Greeks and a stumbling block to the Jews'.

For Gentiles seeking the power that accompanied divine status, the death of Jesus was rather evidence of weak fatuity. For Jews seeking the signs of a true messiah, Jesus' failure to restore the people or to establish the rule of Torah clearly disqualified him from any such claim. And if his life was that of a sinner, his death was one of a criminal cursed by God, for Torah itself declared 'cursed be every one who hangs upon a tree' (Deut. 21:23). The end of Jesus' story, in other words, disconfirmed any claims that might have been made about its significance.

PERSONAL POWER

What made one a Christian in that first generation was the odd insistence that Jesus' significance for the world began after his death, with his resurrection. If we are properly to grasp this, however, we must note carefully what those first believers meant by 'the resurrection'. And we can approach this by stating emphatically what it did *not* mean. It did not mean, as some Gnostic Gospels and the Qur'an dependent on them had it, that Jesus did not die. For Jesus to have escaped death would have been of only temporary interest and only to him. No, Paul is emphatic: 'Christ died' (1 Cor. 15:3). Nor did it mean simply that Jesus had been resuscitated, that is, had experienced what we now call 'clinical death' and then came back for a time. Such things happened frequently in the ancient world as they do in ours, but Lazarus' emergence from the tomb was 'good news' only to him and his family, and only for a short time. The Widow of Naim's son resumed his old life and made his mother glad, but no world-changing religion resulted. Resuscitation is not resurrection. Nor was Jesus' resurrection simply a matter of visions and appearances to selected individuals. Like the stories about an empty tomb, appearance accounts formed an important part of the traditions concerning *how* the resurrected one was experienced by certain 'witnesses' (see 1 Cor. 15:5–8). But the resurrection experience cannot be confined to such sporadic events.

The resurrection faith that gave birth to Christianity was, rather, rooted in a complex combination of experience and conviction. The experience was that of transforming, transcendent, personal power, a power that altered not only the consciousness but the very status of those experiencing it. The symbol for this experience was 'The Holy Spirit'. The term 'spirit' denoted the character of the power: it was not political or military or economic, but rather personal and transformative of human freedom. The term 'holy' designated its origin: it did not come from themselves but from the one who was Other, namely, God. Throughout the New Testament, believers' language about themselves is rooted in this experience. The conviction accompanying this experience is that 'Jesus is Lord'. Jesus is, in other words, alive now in a new and more powerful way after his death than before; he shares, indeed, the very life of God, and makes that life available to humans.

HIS FOLLOWERS – THEIR EVENT

The resurrection was not so much about Jesus as it was about his followers. It was not an event in his history so much as it was an event in theirs. The recognition of his new status as Son of God was immediately connected to the recognition that the power of transformation experienced in community had its origin in him. *This* was the experience powerful enough to draw the disillusioned and disaffected followers of Jesus into a restored people. *This* was the experience that expressed itself in varieties of gifts that upbuilt and nurtured that assembled people. *This* is the experience that radiated across the Mediterranean world in an astonishing proliferation of communities. *This* was the experience and conviction that enabled and necessitated the 'proclamation of the Good

News'. *This* was the experience that empowered those first marginalized and scorned and persecuted to endure in hope through their suffering, knowing that as 'the Christ had to suffer and so enter his glory' (Luke 24:26), so must they.

This, finally, was the experience that made the writing of the New Testament necessary, for the reception of God's Spirit from a crucified Messiah created a cognitive dissonance so profound that those energized by it could not simply live and proclaim the gift, they had also to seek to understand it. The New Testament is such a profoundly gripping set of compositions precisely because it is generated by this powerful collision of experience and symbolic world: the symbols that said Jesus could not be the source of such life, and the experience that testified unequivocally that he was!

READ BACK INTO JESUS' STORY

The process of interpretation sought to resolve the conflict. It did so by showing how Jesus did not, in the eyes of faith, contradict Torah so much as fulfil it. In the process, the resurrection faith was read back into the story of Jesus, so that all the Gospels are suffused with the conviction that the Jesus who wandered Palestine was also the resurrected Son of God. But this retrojection of experience and conviction into narrative had its unintended consequences. The scandal was to some extent lost. Now Jesus appears rather obviously as the Messiah. The mystery is not now his identity but why it should not have been grasped. Increasingly, as in the Gospel of John, Jesus is seen as always having demonstrated what the resurrection experience had first revealed. The culmination of this process was reached in the infancy accounts, not so much those of the canonical Gospels, which retain an essential connection to the 'Good News' of Jesus' death and resurrection, but above all those apocryphal infancy accounts (such as the Infancy Gospel of Thomas) in which Jesus is, from the start, the God-Man.

Classical Christological debates started from the end-point of the earlier process. Christmas, not Easter, is the heart of the

Good News. The incarnation is the mystery of salvation more than the death and resurrection. Once this is accomplished, once Jesus is collapsed into the Christ and the Christ is collapsed into God, then the resurrection becomes just another mystery of the Rosary, another in a series of revelatory moments; no less but also no greater than the annunciation and visitation or transfiguration or ascension. The resurrection, consequently, becomes something that Jesus did, and its significance is what it tells us about who he was all along. But it does so in a no more profound way than his birth. And it certainly has no obvious connection with us.

PUZZLER

The resurrection then becomes something of a puzzler, as debate rages early on over whether it was the 'resurrection of the body', and up to our own day over whether it can be historically verified. And the Holy Spirit, likewise, although elevated to a greater dignity as a member of the Trinity, has a hard time finding a real function in real life.

Most oddly, with the collapse of classical Christology among so many, we find among liberal and liberation versions of Christianity alike a turn to the life of Jesus as a starting point for his significance – precisely where the first outsiders also began! Not surprisingly, such a turn not only yields little agreement (as the proliferation of diverse 'Historical Jesuses' attests), but also precious little to nurture life before God. In such readings, the 'resurrection faith' appears, almost apologetically, not as the most important element in Christian existence, but as its first wrong turn.

The way back is two-fold: first, taking seriously the birth of the Christian religion and the birth of the New Testament out of the matrix of an experience of God mediated through the crucified messiah, and reading those texts for those symptoms; second, searching in our lives together in the Church for the presence of the same personal, transcendent, transforming power in communities, that we can call 'the Holy Spirit', and perhaps on that basis at last again with some conviction preach, 'Jesus is Lord!'

Chapter 6

Discerning God's Word

Preaching in the liturgical assembly is a theological act. Theology in the proper sense is not the study of human opinions but the articulation of faith in the living God. If faith responds to the living God, then faith is an open-ended enterprise, for the living God always moves ahead of us. If theology articulates faith, then theology also is a matter of constant catching up with the work of the God who acts before we do and most often catches us by surprise. The task of theology is to discern and bring to articulate expression the word of God embedded but implicit within human experience, so that the Church can explicitly hear and faithfully respond to that word.

That God speaks to his people is axiomatic for our tradition. So also is the conviction that God's word is powerful and trans-forming. 'The word of God', says the Letter to the Hebrews, 'is living and active, sharper than any two-edged sword, piercing to the division of soul and spirit, and discerning the thoughts and intentions of the heart. And before him no living creature is hidden, but all are open and bare to the eyes of him with whom we have to do' (Heb. 4:12–13).

Understood in this fashion, preaching is a high and awesome responsibility. It is not to be equated with teaching, for in teaching the subject matter is outside of oneself and capable of being controlled. In preaching, the subject matter is very much part of the preacher and calls the one who speaks also into question. It is certainly not to be identified with the delivering of bromide or nosegays of pleasant thoughts. Preaching is not raconteurship, or the recital of charming anecdotes. It is not even the exposition of Scripture. Preaching is not a matter of providing answers. It is, instead, a matter of both preacher and people being brought into question.

THE TASK OF ALL CHRISTIANS

Yet even as we acknowledge that the word of God 'discerns the thoughts and intentions of the heart', we must also confess that the existence and character of that word in specific circumstances is not altogether clear and conspicuous. That God presses upon us in every circumstance of our lives, calling us to response, we all readily agree. But the precise shape of God's word is most often obscure, and requires in turn our discernment.

Such discernment of God's word in the circumstances of human experience is the task of all Christians, but it is given explicit expression by the preacher, just as the response to God's word in the liturgy of prayer and Eucharist gives explicit expression to the inchoate and often incoherent responses of all Christians to the call of God in the circumstances of their lives.

But how can the preacher hear this word of God in order to discern it and give it expression? The sources are almost too many and too rich, for it is the premise of faith in the living God that God is at work in every circumstance of every person's life. The preacher can discern God's work and word first of all in the preacher's own life experience. Nothing is more repulsive than for a sermon to be a preacher's narcissistic 'self-reflection'. But nothing is more alienating than preaching that has not been worked out in fear and trembling through the preacher's own experience. The preacher has nothing to 'tell' others, unless the preacher has first been told; the preacher cannot pose a responsible question to the people unless that question has first been posed by and for the preacher.

Absolutely essential to the preparation for preaching therefore is the prayer of silence. If such prayer is imperative for the life of

44

faith at all – since in it we hear how loud and disruptive our own words are, and allow the silence to still them enough to hear the word God speaks to us through others – it is critical for the preacher. How else but in silence can the preacher hear the word addressed by God through one's own experience? Where else but in silence can the preacher hear the question put to one's own life by this word? Where else but in silence can the preacher let go of the desire to provide an 'answer' for the people and gain the courage to go before them with the 'question' posed by God's word?

A second, astoundingly rich, source for discernment of God's word is the experience of the people. Again the premise: we confess that God is at work, however inarticulately, in the joys and sorrows, the pains and pleasures, the fears and frustrations of everyday life. How else can we discover what God is speaking to us and calling us to, if we close ourselves off from this word? How can the preacher hope to shape a question that fits experience larger than one's own, if the preacher is not also a listener to such human experience, and is its discerner? Not only the preacher's own experience but, even more, the experience of the people must be brought into the process of discernment.

CARE AND CONVERSATION

This points to the theological importance of pastoral care and counselling. Pastoral care and visitation is not simply the expression of love and compassion, though it is certainly and most emphatically that. But it is also the opportunity for the preacher to observe and hear in the specific (and often obscure) details of people's lives the ways in which idolatry and grace, sin and faith, are played out. Likewise, pastoral counselling should be thought of not primarily as a therapeutic exercise, but as a hermeneutical one: counselling is the maieusis of revelation, and the counsellor is one who can help another hear and discern the word of God in the thick textures of everyday life.

The preacher, therefore, is one who prepares for the task of preaching first of all by joining in a complex conversation, where the multiple voices of experience diverge and converge. But even as one's own voice joins the conversation, one is listening for another voice, a voice that speaks only indirectly and obliquely through all these other voices. Such 'overhearing' is a kind of discernment we all practised as children, sitting under the table listening to the grown-ups talk, trying to figure out, through all the complex cross-conversation and laughter, what the real topic was. Now, we seek to 'overhear' the word of God that might emerge from all these voices, which, we are convinced, is the real topic to which we must pay attention and respond.

The preacher also listens with particular care to another set of voices to which the designation 'word of God' has explicitly been attached, the Scriptures. It is important to recognize that Scripture is not a single voice, but is itself a complex conversation. It is a conversation, furthermore, that resulted from a process exactly like the one in which the preacher now participates. The New Testament is the literary residue of a set of conversations within earliest Christianity which sought to interpret the powerful actions of God in the crucified and raised Messiah, Jesus, in the light of the symbols of Torah. Torah itself, as we know, is an older set of conversations concerning the work of God in such paradoxical events as the Exodus, the Exile, and the Return. Neither the texts of Torah nor the texts of the New Testament speak with a single voice. In them, also, the 'word of God' must be discerned by a careful attention to 'the real subject matter' that underlies a bewildering complexity of literary forms, perspectives, and thematic differences.

As essential as the prayer of silence and the practice of pastoral visitation for the preacher's practice of discernment as a con-tinuous theological process is the constant reading of these texts of the Old and New Testaments. Only if the preacher's mind is clothed with these symbols can one's own experience be heard as revelatory of God; only if preachers 'read' the experience of others with the 'mind of Christ' can effective assistance be given to them also to read and express their experience. Only, in other words, if the preacher is always in conversation with these scriptural conversations will the process of listening and speaking about human experience be one that enables the 'word of God' to be spoken.

LECTIONARY PROBLEMS

The explicit turn to sermon preparation is a matter of making this continuous process more explicit and more focused. Now the preacher intensifies the hearing of one's own experience of the week, month, year, searching in the light of prayer and the reading of Scripture for its patterns of idolatry and grace, sin and faith. Now the preacher draws into conversation with the voice of personal experience and reflection all the other voices of the recent weeks, heard in hospital rooms and confessional, spoken in meetings and in passing conversations. And not only the local voices, though these are the most important; the local voices are contextualized by the voices of the headlines and the issues of the region and nation.

The focus is given by the specific lectionary texts assigned for the day. Using the lectionary is theologically appropriate, for it enables us to respond to the words of Scripture as 'other', and prevents us from finding texts that suit the message we want to give. Being forced to deal with texts that come to us from the outside enables us to 'listen' to them as we do to the other voices to which we listen as we try to overhear the word God speaks to the people.

The lectionary also poses some real problems for the preacher. For one thing, although we can *functionally* regard these texts as 'other', we know full well that lectionaries too are the works of human hands. Sometimes, the texts from Old and New Testaments come together coincidentally. Other times, we can see the ways in which the selection of the texts has been informed by the desire to make a certain point or reinforce a certain theme. This artificial 'closing' of the Scripture, in which a text from the Old Testament is 'answered' by a text from the New Testament, requires the preacher's energy and intelligence to reopen, if the texts are to be allowed to pose a question and not a pre-packaged answer. The preacher must resist the easy route of proclaiming what the texts obviously invite, for to follow that path would be not to discern the word, but to manipulate and retail it.

Another difficulty presented by the lectionary is that the texts do not occur in their scriptural context but in tiny fragments. For those of us whose only training in Scripture has been through the historical-critical approach, with its emphasis on exegeting passages 'in their context', this arrangement leaves us feeling irresponsible. Small wonder that many conscientious preachers think their job has been done when they subject their hearers to an earnest 'contextualization' of each passage in turn: 'here is what Paul was trying to tell the Corinthians . . .', 'this is what Isaiah's situation was . . .' But the Scripture is read in the assembly not so that we can find out what it meant back then, but so that we can hear how God's word challenges us today.

OFFENSIVE?

Preachers need to become more comfortable with the 'conversational model' of hermeneutics I have been sketching, and recognize that the fragmentary state of these texts is not unlike the fragmentary patches of conversation heard in pastoral visitations and counselling and reading and prayer. What is needed is to bring these scriptural fragments into play with all those other voices in an even broader conversation.

The preacher might begin by reading the various pieces of the Scripture texts out loud repeatedly. How do they sound in the midst of all the other voices the preacher carries around in the head and heart? It is rare when some sort of connection does not occur, some sort of allusion does not offer itself. Most of all, what is it in any of these texts the preacher does *not* want to hear, or think about, or preach? What is it that the preacher finds offensive? This is the most important clue for interpretation and discernment. The creative preacher can begin from such a point, recognizing that the text is touching on something either the preacher's voice or the voices of the people need to hear in direct proportion to their desire not to hear it.

A THEOLOGICAL ACT

It is from such a starting-point that the preacher can begin to pursue the process of discernment. Was the feeling or sense accurate? Where does it lead, what is the implication? Does the experience of God in this community confirm or disconfirm this text? Then what should we do in either case? Does the text challenge the assumption of my voice and the voices I hear among my people of how God is acting because of how God *must* act? Then what should we do about those assumptions?

As these questions are asked, then the texts are probed more diligently and vigorously in terms of their original scriptural context. Is the sense of these voices in combination one that can responsibly be attributed to them in their canonical context? If not, do these voices in combination teach us something in the way they converge or collide that none of them could individually, in their canonical context?

These questions should move toward a question that truly addresses the experience of the preacher and the people alike. How much better it is for the preacher to provide one legitimate, powerful question out of this struggle with the many voices, than any number of pat or pre-packaged answers.

The sermon should be short, and it should be written. It should be written in utterly simple and non-pretentious language. It should be written because the discernment of the word of God is not a matter for carelessness. If the time is short (as it should be), and if the word has posed a real question for the preacher and the people (as we hope it has), then writing is imperative. Among other things, writing enables the preacher also to *listen* to what is being said.

Is this approach to preaching messy? You bet. Hard to control? Yes. Anxiety-provoking, as the time to speak approaches? Absolutely. All of which is to indicate that something living and real and exciting is happening. Preaching is in danger of becoming a theological act.

Chapter 7

Jesus and the Little Children

A GOSPEL PERSPECTIVE ON THE CHURCH SCANDAL

The crisis in the Church caused by the sexual abuse of children by clergy will not quickly disappear, because the crisis is not really about sex so much as about the abuse of power. Priests who used their position to sexually seduce or assault young people abused their power. Bishops who hid those crimes and placed priests where they could continue their predatory behaviour abused their power. This is the point that all laity get and few priests and bishops seem to grasp.

We all fail sexually. And because the flesh is weak, we find it easy to forgive each other (if not always ourselves) when we have given in to sexual temptation. But even the simplest among us knows that there is a difference in gravity between masturbation and fornication, between fornication and adultery, a difference that has to do not with the nature of the sexual act or the nature of sexual pleasure, but with the nature of the relationships involved. Adultery is worse than fornication because it betrays the covenant between persons.

Clergy preying sexually on the young is on another scale altogether. It makes no difference whether we speak of paedophilia in the clinical sense or other forms of sexual seduction and assault. Whether stemming from a clinical pathology or simple lust, the wrong involved is not sex but the breaking of boundaries between adult and youth, the betrayal of trust between the representative of the Gospel and an innocent believer who placed his or her trust in that representative.

The crisis in the Church will not quickly pass away, because the patterns of authority within the Church that have enabled and abetted such behavior seem utterly resistant to change. All signs indicate that the Roman Catholic Church will not change its requirement of an all-male, celibate, priesthood. And there-fore the patterns of abuse will continue. This is not because celibacy in itself is the issue, but because celibate clergy form a caste whose formation and way of life keep its members from fully appreciating what every parent understands, namely the particular horror of destroying the innocence of a child.

Priests and bishops don't get it, I think, because they live in a societal subgroup that is like that of the police. They are defined by their difference from, and authority over, lay people. And like the police, their first loyalty is to each other rather than to the laity. Unless women are ordained, unless married males are ordained, it is unlikely that the chasm between the perceptions of the laity on this matter and those of the clergy will be bridged.

The crisis, in a word, is not simply about the sexual morality of certain priests but about the morality of the entire authority structure (and practice) of the Church. It will not be resolved by strengthening the commitment to celibacy, for it is not lack of chastity that is the real issue.

It can only be resolved by the church's profound conversion of mind and practice to a fuller accord with the mind and practice of Jesus Christ.

It is impossible to read the Gospels – especially those of Mark, Matthew, and Luke – without noticing what special attention Jesus gives to children and to the 'little ones' of the earth whom children so perfectly exemplify: those who are weak, vulnerable, needy, and demanding. The simple fact that Jesus 'saw' children precisely as children, and saw them in particular need of care, means that Jesus was distinctive among the great men of antiquity, and indeed among the great leaders of every age.

In the present crisis, it may be helpful to remind ourselves of Jesus and the little children, to remember what Jesus himself said about scandal. We can do this by reading through that portion of the Gospel of Mark following the story of the transfiguration (Mark 9:1–13), when Jesus and his chosen followers begin a journey toward Jerusalem.

This part of the story is dominated by Jesus' predictions of his suffering and death, and the instruction of his disciples on what it means to follow him and what it means to be a leader. Children figure into these themes in fascinating and important ways.

THE BOY WITH THE UNCLEAN SPIRIT

Coming down from the Mount of Transfiguration, Jesus and his closest followers encounter other disciples who had been trying to drive an unclean spirit out of a boy. The father approaches Jesus and reports how the disciples were unable to drive the demon out. When the boy is brought to Jesus, he falls into a violent seizure. Jesus inquires of the father concerning the son's situation: 'How long has this been happening to him?' (9:21), and listens to the parent's heartbreaking report of how his child's life – and his own – was being destroyed by this malignant power (9:21–22). When Jesus declares that all things are possible to the one who believes, the man memorably replies, 'I believe, help my unbelief!' At the command of Jesus, the spirit departs the child, but so violently that the child lies on the ground as one dead. Jesus 'took him by the hand, and lifted him up, and he was able to stand' (9:27).

We are told nothing in this story about the age of the boy. But it is appropriate to call him a child, for whatever his age, his affliction makes him still under the care of his parent. The story does not sentimentalize. Just the opposite: it shows us how fragile and perilous the life of this (or any) child is, and how devastating for the entire family is the destructive force at work in him. Mark portrays a Jesus who healed first by his seeing and hearing the child and parent in their relationship, and then touched the child, not for self-gratification, but to restore the child to his parent and, even more, to himself.

ACCEPTING THE CHILD IS ACCEPTING JESUS

As Mark's story progresses, the reader slowly becomes aware that the evangelist is drawing a sharp contrast between the attitudes and behaviour of Jesus and those of his chosen followers. The contrast is the more pointed because the reader also knows that these inadequate disciples represent the very figures who will be the leaders of the community after the death and resurrection of Jesus. The contrast becomes poignant when it is displayed in terms of attitudes and actions toward children.

Immediately after the healing of the boy, Jesus announces for a second time that he will be betrayed and will be killed (9:31). Although the disciples do not understand, they are afraid to ask him (9:32). Instead, they fall into a dispute over who among them was the greatest (9:34)! The contrast between the suffering messiah and the pretentiously self-involved followers could scarcely be more obvious.

Jesus responds to this remarkable display of arrogance by announcing – to the twelve – a different standard of measurement among his followers: 'Whoever wants to be first must be last of all and servant of all' (9:35). Then he 'took a little child and put it among them, and taking it in his arms, he said, "Whoever welcomes one such child in my name welcomes me, and whoever welcomes me welcomes not me, but the one who sent me" ' (9:35).

The precise connection between Jesus' gesture and his words is not entirely clear. The child is placed among them first to illustrate the simple point that among them, leadership is to be expressed by humility and service. But Jesus' next words push beyond that to say something important about the way in which children themselves are received. It is not merely that leaders in the church are to be humble servants. The way they respond to children is a measure of their response to God. If they welcome a little one in Jesus' name, they welcome Jesus, and thereby also welcome God.

SCANDAL AND THE MILLSTONE

The corollary of that proposition, to be sure, is that rejecting children is rejecting Jesus and rejecting God. What, then, would the abusing and corrupting of children mean? The very next passage takes up that point.

Once more, Mark depicts the arrogance of Jesus' followers. Their notion of authority is control over others: they seek to stop 'unauthorized' exorcists who were casting out demons in Jesus' name (9:38). Jesus rejects such an understanding of authority. The point is not whether the work of God is under the control of the apostles, but whether it liberates humans: 'whoever is not against us is for us. For truly I tell you, whoever gives you a cup of water to drink because you bear the name of Christ will by no means lose the reward' (9:41). Here is a neat reversal of the twelve's expectations: they are not dispensers of favours, they are the recipients of gifts from others, whom they cannot control.

But Jesus then returns to the subject of children, and all other 'little ones' for whom these leaders-in-training are to exercise care, with powerfully prophetic words that ought to strike the ears of the contemporary church with great force:

> If any of you put a stumbling block (*skandalon*) before one of these little ones who believe in me, it would be better for you if a great millstone were hung around your neck and you were thrown into the sea.
>
> (9:42)

The Greek term for 'stumbling block' is the one that has made its way into English as 'scandal.' We speak of the 'scandal' in the Church as though it were a matter of bad publicity or shame. And bishops protected predatory priests and exposed children to further harm in order to avoid the 'scandal' that would result from dealing with crime (and sin) as crime (and sin). But scandal in the New Testament means something far more serious. Scandal means causing the destruction of another through one's own actions (see 1 Cor. 8:9–13). The 'scandal' in the Church today has nothing to do with publicity. It has everything to do with the Church's willingness to protect the predators who destroy the lives of children. How? Not simply by exposing them to sexual activity before they are ready and through seduction or rape, but by utterly betraying the fragile web of trust of 'these little ones who believe in me'.

These are the most powerful words of moral repugnance found in Jesus' mouth. The merciful saviour, declaring it better that an adult leader be drowned with a millstone around the neck, than that such a leader betray the trust placed in him!

Jesus' following words ought also to have been heard by those who refused to act decisively when they became aware of such systemic and long-standing corruption. The singular 'you' in these lines can be read as plural, and applied to the Church as such:

> If your hand causes you to stumble, cut it off; it is better for you to enter life maimed than to have two hands and go to hell, to the unquenchable fire. And if your foot causes you to stumble, cut it off; it is better for you to enter life lame than to have two feet and be thrown into hell. And if your eye causes you to stumble, tear it out; it is better for you to enter life with one eye than to have two eyes and to be thrown into hell.
>
> (9:43–47)

If we take Jesus' words seriously, we must conclude that it is better for the Church to endure any damage that shame might bring it by removing predatory priests and protecting the innocent, than to lose its integrity and with it the trust of its own people. A saying that follows is pertinent: 'Salt is good. But if salt has lost its saltiness, how can you season it?' (9:49).

CHILDREN AND THE KINGDOM OF GOD

Following immediately on Jesus' words against divorce (10:2–11), Mark reports another striking incident involving children. This time people were bringing children to Jesus so that he might touch them, while the disciples 'spoke sternly to them'. Once more, the soon-to-be-leaders of the community are portrayed as deaf to the concerns of parents. Mark says that Jesus was 'indignant' at this, saying to the disciples:

> Let the little children come to me, for it is to such as these the kingdom of God belongs. Truly I tell you, whoever does not receive the kingdom as a little child will never enter it.
>
> (10:14–15)

We must note carefully exactly what Jesus says in Mark's version of the story. He does not say that the disciples must become like children. Rather the story and the saying in combination clearly mean that *the way one receives children is the way one receives the kingdom of God.* As in the earlier story, welcoming children *is* the measure of one's reception of God's rule. We can extrapolate: the way one treats children is a measure of how seriously one lives under the rule of God. And we can apply this to the present behaviour of the hierarchy: the way children are put in jeopardy in order to save the reputation of the institution is a clear statement of how the hierarchy understands God's Rule as stated by Jesus – not at all.

POWER AND SERVICE

The final passage of which we need reminding also follows a prediction of his suffering by Jesus, and another dispute over authority among his followers (10:32–41). This time, James and John want to sit at Jesus' side as rulers, and the other disciples – apparently out of envy – grow angry with them. Jesus does not promise them a place of honour but only a share in his sufferings (10:36–40). Then, in a final reminder to his disciples (and the readers of the Gospel) Jesus summarizes the character of leadership within his community as a continuation of his own life of sacrificial self-giving:

You know that among the Gentiles those whom they recognize as their rulers lord it over them, and their great ones are tyrants over them. But it is not so among you; but whoever wishes to become great among you must be your servant, and whoever wishes to be first among you must be slave of all. For the Son of Man came not to be served but to serve, and to give his life as a ransom for many.

(10:42–45)

Jesus emphatically rejects the attitudes of ambition and self-serving that he sees among those whom he chose to lead his community. As he moves toward his own death, he summons them to a higher vision of leadership that corresponds to the pattern of his own life: they must be small and they must be servants.

CONVERSION MEANS CHANGE

In the face of public scrutiny, the Catholic hierarchy has scrambled to contain the damage it has done, but there is little evidence that it has actually understood the damage that it has done. Establishing zero-tolerance policies for predators is scarcely a heroic response, yet even it has been resisted by the Vatican. And despite the gestures of apology and sorrow enunciated by various bishops, it is difficult to avoid the impression that this is largely an exercise in the protocol of self-prostration that is now required of the powerful when they have been caught colluding in corruption. I have yet to see any Bishop state clearly how and why the predatory behavior of the clergy and the self-protecting cover-up by bishops is an abuse of power that requires both real change in the way things are done in the Church, and a real change in the people who do things in the Church. I have yet to hear a bishop show how these patterns of the abuse of power stand condemned by the Gospel, by the plain and forceful words of Jesus. Perhaps it has been some time since they have actually read these words. Perhaps the way to change is through reminder, and the means of reminding is reading.

Chapter 8

Scripture and Discernment:
the Case of Homosexuality

Homosexuality as an issue internal to the life of the Church poses a fundamental challenge not only to moral discernment and pastoral care (the two aspects touched on in the recent *Catechism of the Catholic Church*) but to the self-understanding of the Church as at once inclusive ('catholic') and separate ('holy'). The question is not only how we feel or think or act concerning homosexuality, but also how those feelings, thoughts, and actions relate to the canonical texts which we take as normative for our lives together. Homosexuality in the Church presents a hermeneutical problem.

The present chapter has the modest goal of clearing some space for debate and discernment by setting out what seem to be appropriate boundary markers for what promises to be a long and difficult discussion. I proceed by staking out three basic premises concerning ecclesial hermeneutics, and then a number of theses pertinent to the issue of homosexuality.

I take it as a given, first, that any process of discernment within the Church takes as its fundamental framework the Irenaean triad of ecclesial self-definition: the canon of Scripture, the rule of faith, and the teaching authority of bishops. To step outside this framework is to shift the debate to other grounds entirely. Conservatism in commitment to canon, creed, and council is paradoxically the necessary condition for genuine freedom in scriptural interpretation.

Second, I take it as basic that hermeneutics involves the complex task of negotiating normative texts and continuing human experiences. Within the faith community, this means an openness to the ways in which God's revelation continues in human experience as well as a deep commitment to the conviction that such revelation, while often, at first, perceived as dissonant with the symbols of Scripture, will, by God's grace directing human fidelity, be seen as consonant with those symbols and God's own fidelity. Essentially, however, the call of faith is to the living God whose revelation continues, rather than to *our previous understanding* of the texts. Faith in the living God seeks understanding; theological understanding does not define faith or the living God.

My third premise is that Scripture does not characteristically speak with a single voice. Rather, as an anthology of compositions it contains an irreducible and precious pluralism of 'voices', shaped by literary genre, theme, and perspective. The *authority* of these texts, furthermore, is most properly distinguished in terms of their function. Their highest authority is found in their capacity to reliably 'author' Christian identity. Almost as important is the way in which these texts 'authorize' a certain freedom in interpretation, by presenting a model of how Torah was reinterpreted in the light of new experiences. A third sort of authority is important but not as fundamental. The Scripture contains a wide range of 'authorities' in the sense of *auctoritates*, or 'opinions', not on all the subjects we could desire, but on many of great significance. Responsible hermeneutics claims the 'freedom of the children of God' authorized by the New Testament, and seeks to negotiate the various 'voices/ authorities' within the texts in an effort to conform to that 'mind of Christ' (1 Cor. 2:16) that is the authentic form of Christian identity which those texts are, through the power of the Holy Spirit, capable of 'authoring'.

I would like to think that these three premises, though perhaps nontraditional in formulation, are in essence profoundly Catholic, fairly and accurately representing not only the implications of the New Testament's own origin and canonization, but also of much loyal and creative interpretation within the tradition.

Before moving to the specific case of homosexuality, it might be helpful to amplify slightly two aspects of these premises which without explication might appear careless, if not cavalier. The first concerns the experience of God in human lives. Nothing could be more offensive than to challenge tradition on the basis of casual or unexamined experience, as though God's revelation were obvious or easy, or reducible to popularity polls. The call to the discernment of human experience is not a call to carelessness, but its opposite; it is a call to the rigorous asceticism of attentiveness. I repeat: an appeal to some populist claim such as 'everyone does it', or 'surveys indicate' is theologically meaningless. What counts is whether *God* is up to something in human lives. Discernment of experience in this sense is for the detection of good news in surprising places, not for the disguising of old sins in novel faces.

Yet it is important to assert that God *does*, on the record, act in surprising and unanticipated ways, and upsets human perceptions of God's scriptural precedents. The most fundamental instance for the very existence of Christianity is the unexpected, crucified, and raised Messiah, Jesus. A considerable amount of what we call the New Testament derives from the attempt to resolve the cognitive dissonance between the experience of Jesus as the source of God's Holy Spirit, and the text of Torah that disqualifies him from that role, since, 'cursed be every one that hangs upon a tree' (Deut. 23:21; *see* Gal. 3:13).

Another example is the spread of the gospel to the Gentiles. It is easy for us at this distance, and with little understanding of the importance of the body language of table fellowship, to take for granted such a breaking of precedent that allowed Gentiles to share fully in the life of the Messianic community without being circumcised or practicing observance of Torah. Good for us, also, therefore, to read Acts 10–15 to see just how agonizing and difficult a task it was for that first generation of Christians to allow their perception of God's activity to change their perceptions, and use that new experience as the basis for reinterpreting Scripture.

The second aspect of the premises I want to amplify slightly is the requirement for responsible hermeneutics to take every voice of Scripture seriously. I spoke of the *auctoritates* as diverse and sometimes contradictory. But every ecclesial decision to live by one rather than another of these voices, to privilege one over another, to suppress one in order to live by another, must be willing to state the grounds of that decision, and demonstrate how 'the experience of God and the more fundamental principles of 'the mind of Christ' and 'freedom of the children of God' (principles also rooted in the authority of the text) legitimate the distance between ecclesial decision and a clear statement of Scripture. Do we allow divorce (even if we don't openly call it that) when Jesus forbade it? We must be willing to support our decision by an appeal, not simply to changing circumstances, but to a deeper wisdom given by the Spirit into the meaning of human covenant, and therefore a better understanding of the sayings of Jesus. This is never easy. It is sometimes – as in the case of taking oaths and vows – not even possible. But it is the task of responsible ecclesial hermeneutics.

How does this approach provide a context for the hermeneutics of homosexuality? First, it cautions us against trying to suppress biblical texts which condemn homosexual behavior (Lev. 18:22; Wisd. 14:26; Rom. 1:26–7; 1 Cor. 6:9) or to make them say something other than what they say. I think it fair to conclude that early Christianity knew about homosexuality as it was practised in Graeco-Roman culture, shared Judaism's association of it with the 'abominations' of idolatry, and regarded it as incompatible with life in the Kingdom of God. These *auctoritates* emphatically define homosexuality as a vice, and they cannot simply be dismissed.

Second, however, Scripture itself 'authorizes' us to exercise the freedom of the children of God in our interpretation of such passages. We are freed, for example, to evaluate the relative paucity of such condemnations. Compared to the extensive and detailed condemnation of economic oppression at virtually every level of tradition, the off-handed rejection of homosexuality appears instinctive and relatively unreflective. We are freed as well to assess the contexts of the condemnations: the rejection of homosexuality, as of other sexual sins, is connected to the incompatibility of *porneia* with life in the Kingdom. We can further observe that the flat rejection of *porneia* (any form of sexual immorality) is more frequent and general than any of its specific manifestations. We are freed, finally, to consider the grounds on which the texts seem to include homosexuality within *porneia*, namely that it is 'against nature', an abomination offensive to God's created order.

Such considerations, in turn, provide an opening for a conversation between our human experience (including our religious experience) and the texts of our tradition. Does our experience now support or challenge the assumption that homosexuality is, simply and without exception, an 'offence against nature'? Leviticus and Paul considered homosexuality a vice because they assumed it was a deliberate choice that 'suppressed the truth about God'. Is that a fair assessment of homosexuality as we have come to understand it? It is, of course grossly distorting to even talk about 'homosexuality' as though one clearly definable thing were meant. But many of us who have gay and lesbian friends and relatives have arrived with them at the opposite conclusion: for many persons the acceptance of their homosexuality *is* an acceptance of creation as it applies to them. It is emphatically *not* a vice that is chosen. If this conclusion is correct, what is the hermeneutical implication?

Another order of questions concerns the connection of homosexuality to *porneia*. The Church, it is clear, cannot accept *porneia*. But what is the essence of 'sexual immorality'? In the moral quality of sexual behaviour defined biologically in terms of the use of certain body parts, or is it defined in terms of personal commitment and attitudes? Is not *porneia* essentially sexual activity that ruptures covenant, just as *castitas* is sexual virtue within or outside marriage because it is sexuality in service to convenant?

If sexual virtue and vice are defined covenantally rather than biologically, then it is possible to place homosexual and heterosexual activity in the same context. Certainly, the church must reject the *porneia* which glorifies sex for its own sake, indulges in promiscuity, destroys the bonds of commitment, and seduces the innocent. Insofar as a 'gay lifestyle' has these connotations, the Church must emphatically and always say 'no' to it. But the Church must say 'no' with equal emphasis to the heterosexual '*Playboy/Cosmo* life-style' version. In both cases, also, the Church can acknowledge that human sexual activity, while of real and great significance, is not wholly determinative of human existence or worth, and can perhaps begin to ask whether the Church's concentration on sexual behaviour corresponds proportionally to the modest emphasis placed by Scripture.

The harder question, of course, is whether the Church can recognize the possibility of homosexual committed and convenantal love, in the way that it recognizes such sexual/personal love in the sacrament of marriage. This is a harder question because it pertains not simply to moral attitudes or pastoral care, but to the social symbolization of the community. The issue here is analogous to the one facing earliest Christianity after Gentiles started being converted. Granted that they had been given the Holy Spirit, could they be accepted into the people of God just as they were, or must they first 'become Jewish' by being circumcised and obeying all the ritual demands of Torah? Remember, please, the stakes: the Gentiles were 'by nature' unclean, and were 'by practice' polluted by idolatry. We are obsessed by the sexual dimensions of the body. The first-century Mediterranean world was obsessed by the social implications of food and table-fellowship. The decision to let the Gentiles in 'as is' and to establish a more inclusive form of table-fellowship, we should note, came into direct conflict with the accepted interpretation of Torah and what God wanted of humans.

The decision, furthermore, was not easy to reach. Paul's Letter to the Galatians suggests some of the conflict it generated. Even the irenic Luke devotes five full chapters of Acts (10–15) to the account of how the community caught up with God's intentions, stumbling every step of the way through confusion, doubt, challenge, disagreements, divisions and debate. Much suffering had to be endured before the implications of Peter's question, 'If then God gave the same gift to them as he gave to us when we believed in the Lord Jesus Christ, who was I that could withstand God?' (Acts 11:17), could be fully answered: 'We believe that we [Jews] shall be saved through the grace of the Lord Jesus, just as they [Gentiles] will' (Acts 15:11).

The grounds of the Church's decision then was the work that God was doing among the Gentiles, bringing them to salvation through faith. On the basis of this experience of God's work, the Church made bold to reinterpret Torah, finding there unexpected legitimation for its fidelity to God's surprising ways (Acts 15:15–18). How was that work of God made known to the Church? Through the narratives of faith related by Paul and Barnabas and Peter, their personal testimony of how 'signs and wonders' had been worked among the Gentiles (Acts 15:4, 6–11, 12–13).

Such witness is what the church now needs from homosexual Christians. Are homosexuality and holiness of life compatible? Is homosexual convenantal love according to 'the mind of Christ', an authentic realization of that Christian identity authored by the Holy Spirit, and therefore 'authored' as well by the Scripture despite the 'authorities' speaking against it? The Church can discern this only on the basis of faithful witness. The burden of proof required to overturn scriptural precedents is heavy, but it is a burden that has been borne before. The Church cannot, should not, define itself in response to political pressure or popularity polls. But it is called to discern the work of God in human lives and adapt its self-understanding in response to the work of God. Inclusivity must follow from evidence of holiness; are there narratives of homosexual holiness to which we must begin to listen?

Chapter 9

The Biblical Foundations
of Matrimony

The Christian sacraments sanctify the moments of ordinary life and make them extraordinary through the mystery of Christ. The natural impulse to mark the transition to a new community by a ritual of initiation becomes the sacrament of baptism when joined to the death and resurrection of Jesus. The catechumen does not simply join a new group but enters into new life. The natural tendency to share food becomes the sacrament of the Eucharist through association with Jesus' final meal with his followers. Christians celebrate not simply their fellowship with each other but also their fellowship with the risen Lord Jesus Christ. The sacraments punctuate our ordinary human existence with the reminder that the simple ways in which we join ourselves to each other point also to a larger drama in which we are joined to God. The sacraments mark the moments of creation as glimpses of the new creation.

ORDER OF THE FIRST CREATION

Nothing would seem to be more natural than the joining of male and female in sexual union. That is certainly the view of Genesis, which speaks of God's image as borne by male and female together (Gen. 1:27) and approvingly notes how those who are 'bone of bone' and 'flesh of flesh' seek to be bound to each other: 'Therefore a man leaves his father and his mother and clings to his wife, and they become one flesh' (Gen. 2:23–24). Paul refers to this same Genesis passage when speaking about human sexuality (1 Cor. 6:16; Eph. 5:31). In this sense, marriage is part of the order of the first creation. It is as ancient as humanity. Throughout the Old Testament, marriage is assumed to be the calling of every human being. Virginity is tragic; infertility, a curse. God's blessings are given through the process of procreation.

Because the coming together of woman and man is so natural a part of creation and declared by God with the rest of creation as 'good' (Gen. 1:31), the Old Testament pays relatively little attention to the sexual or affective aspects of marriage as such, focusing instead on the command given to the first couple to 'be fruitful and multiply and fill the earth and subdue it' (Gen. 1:28). Especially after God declares to Abraham the intention of making one family (Abraham's seed) the means by which all humans would be blessed (12:1–3), the biblical story is preoccupied with issues of fertility and descent (see, for example, Gen. 15:1–6; 16:1–6; 17:1–8; 21:1–14; 25:19–34; 27:18–29). The laws written for the people's observance in the land of Israel likewise concentrated on issues of descent through the male seed and the preservation of the chosen people through marriage and childbearing within the proper boundaries (Num. 25:6–15; Deut. 7:3). Adultery and the coveting of another's wife is forbidden (Exod. 20:17; Deut. 22:22), as is the marrying of foreign women. The male perspective in all of this is dominant. Thus, the man can divorce a woman who displeases him (Deut. 24:1–4). And while Proverbs describes the ideal wife (Prov. 31:10–31), it does not mention the ideal husband.

COVENANT PARTNER

Because the bond between woman and man was essentially a covenant, however, it could also serve to symbolize the covenant between Israel and the Lord. The analogy is clear: the Lord chose Israel as covenant partner. Obeying other gods is breaking covenant. And since the 'foreign women' that Israelites might marry would also bring their 'foreign gods' into Israel, it was almost inevitable that religious apostasy would be expressed in terms of adultery. The use of sexual (and specifically marriage) symbolism for the relationship between the Lord and Israel is a feature especially of the prophetic literature, although it can be detected in Wisdom writings as well (for example, Proverbs 1–9). Hosea, Jeremiah and Isaiah all imagine the bond between Israel and God in terms of the forming and the breaking and the restoration of a marriage covenant (Hos. 1:2–3:5; Jer. 2:23–25; 3:1–23; Isa. 50:1–2; 54:5–8). It is a powerful symbolism. When used negatively, it can also be frightening, as when Ezekiel portrays the Lord in terms that strongly evoke a violent and abusive husband (Ezekiel 16).

The Old Testament has a concern for progeny and property as well as for the powerful symbolism of covenant. Only in a few places do we spot some of the playfulness and pleasure of sexual life, some of the joy of this natural covenant between man and woman. The supreme example is the Song of Solomon, which unabashedly celebrates erotic love, without even a mention of marriage. Small wonder that commentators (both Jewish and Christian) read the Song in terms of the covenant between Israel and the Lord.

MARRIAGE IN THE NEW TESTAMENT

In the New Testament the absolute status of marriage is challenged because of the radical character of the Christian experience. First, Jesus himself lived a radical lifestyle and died violently at an early age without having married or begotten children. Second, Jesus' resurrection as 'life-giving spirit' (1 Cor. 15:45) made the reception of God's blessings not dependent on biological fertility but on the power of the Spirit. Third, the expectation that 'the frame of this world is passing away' (1 John 2:17) made the natural order relative rather than absolute. The resurrection experience is eschatological. It inaugurates a 'new creation' (2 Cor. 5:17). Of this, the New Testament writings are certain. But they are less certain how this new creation affects marriage. The New Testament is ambivalent about this basic human relationship in a way that the Old Testament is not.

Thus, we see Jesus, on one side, call for a commitment in marriage (on the basis of Genesis 1!) that excludes all divorce (Mark 10:2–12; Luke 16:18) – a command with which the early Church clearly struggled (1 Cor. 7:10–16; Matt. 5:31–32; 19:3–9). But on the other side, he calls his disciples to abandon their families for the sake of the kingdom of God, and he speaks of those who are 'eunuchs for the kingdom of God' (Matt. 19:10–12). And he rejects the Sadducees who pin everything on marriage by declaring that those 'in the resurrection of the dead neither marry nor are given in marriage' (Luke 20:34–35). Yet, Jesus also continues the image of Scripture when he speaks of himself as the bridegroom (Luke 5:33–35). The two dimensions merge in John's account of Jesus' miracle at the wedding feast at Cana (John 2:1–11). He blesses the first creation by his presence, but he symbolizes the inauguration of the new creation by changing the water into wine.

COMPLEXITY AND AMBIGUITY

The same complex attitude toward marriage appears in the other New Testament compositions. On one side, we find the repeated approval of marriage as God's good creation (1 Tim. 4:3–5) to be lived by husband and wife in fidelity and holiness (see 1 Thess. 4:3–6; 1 Cor. 7:1–16; Col. 3:18; Eph. 5:22–30; Heb. 13:4). On the other side, we find that an appreciation for the new creation through Christ complicates things. Paul does not regard virginity and widowhood as the tragedies that they were in Israel. God's Holy Spirit can give life and blessing quite apart from marriage and childbearing. Indeed, Paul argues that, 'in the present circumstances', a single life has the advantage of enabling a commitment to the work of the Lord that is unencumbered by the (legitimate) anxiety that married people have toward spouses and children (1 Cor. 7:17–40).

The same ambiguity is found in the two passages (outside the Gospels) where the marriage imagery of the prophets occurs. In Revelation 14:3–5, the 144,000 who sing a new song to the Lamb before the throne 'have not defiled themselves with women, for they are virgins'; and in the final vision, the Church is 'the bride, the wife of the Lamb' (Rev. 21:9): 'the spirit and the bride say, "Come" ' (22:17). Here, the symbolism of Christ and the Church as bridegroom and bride simply displaces the human reality of marriage. But in Paul's Letter to the Ephesians, that imagery serves to strengthen the marriage between real women and men. After addressing the attitudes of mutual submission between spouses – and the particular obligation of the husband to give his life for his spouse 'just as Christ loved the church and gave himself up for her' (Eph. 5:25), Paul provides the clearest basis in the New Testament for the sacramental character of the human institution of marriage. Quoting the Genesis text about the two becoming one flesh (Gen. 2:24), Paul says, 'This is a great mystery, and I am applying it to Christ and the Church' (Eph. 5:32). Placed in the overall argument of Ephesians, he means that, just as the reconciliation between Jew and Gentile in the Church symbolizes the peace that Jesus had brought about through his death and resurrection (Eph. 2:1–10), so does the loving relationship between husband and wife provide a sign *to* the Church of its own truest identity.

THEOLOGY OF MARRIAGE

The tension within the New Testament between marriage and virginity was quickly lost. Subsequent generations of Christians – for a variety of reasons – so favoured virginity as the preferred mode of Christian life that marriage sometimes seemed, at most, something allowed rather than encouraged. The Church has, as a result, never really developed a satisfactory theology of marriage. The theology of marriage has far too often been a combination of legal norms and moral strictures written by people with no real knowledge of the actual sacrament, whose ministers are the woman and man themselves. Here is a case where the testimony of Scripture can and should be opened up to new examination and new evaluation by the experience and wisdom of those who have lived out this sacrament, and who can provide living witness to the ways in which the ordinary and often humdrum realities of married life – its pains and also its pleasures – are sanctified and deepened by the mystery that is Christ and the Church.

Chapter 10

Reconciliation in the New Testament

The mystery of what God has done for us through the life, death, and resurrection of Jesus Christ is impossible adequately to express in words. No single set of ideas or images captures every aspect of the mystery. The New Testament compositions themselves use a variety of images and metaphors to express something of what God has accomplished among us. The New Testament speaks, for example, of being saved, or redeemed, or liberated, terms that suggest rescue from slavery and deliverance to freedom. Other expressions derive from a forensic context: sins are forgiven, people are declared righteous. Still others come from the cultic life of Israel: expiation for sins, atonement, purification, sanctification.

Each of these sets of metaphors has its own logic, drawn from the cultural context in which it originated. The language of justification/righteousness, which assumes the setting of a law-court, is distinct from that of expiation, which assumes the ritual of the day of atonement, with its sprinkling of blood on the altar. What Christian theology has gained by trying to arrange these metaphors systematically (first atonement, then righteousness, then sanctification) is less valuable than what it has lost, namely the sense that the mystery can be named in all these distinct and non reducible ways while yet escaping complete definition.

Distinctive though each metaphor is, they share three characteristics. First, each expresses the change in humans from one state or condition to another, from a minus (slavery, death, sin) to a plus (freedom, life, spirit). Second, each metaphor makes clear that it is God who has brought about the change for humans. They do not forgive their own sins but have them forgiven by God; they do not liberate themselves but are freed by God. Third, Jesus is always the agent by which God has brought about this change: he is the expiation for sins, he is the one who saves, he is the one who establishes humans as righteous before God.

THE LANGUAGE OF RECONCILIATION

The language of reconciliation is also used for the mystery of God's work for humans in Jesus Christ. It is distinctive on several counts. First, the Greek terms *katallassein* and *katallagē* that 'reconcile' translates are often used in ordinary literature to mean simply to 'change' or 'alter' something (like currency), and it occurs with this non-theological sense in the Septuagint of Jeremiah 31:39 and Isaiah 9:5. As in our contemporary world, however, language about reconciliation applied in antiquity mainly to the political realm, where it signified the 'change in relations' between parties: whereas they formerly were estranged, they are now 'reconciled.' In his single non-theological use of the term, Paul gives us a glimpse at the options: in his discussion of marriage, Paul says that the wife should not separate from her husband, but if she does, she should either remain unmarried or be reconciled to her husband (1 Cor. 7:11).

Second, this language is virtually absent from the Old Testament. The only place in the (Catholic) Old Testament where reconciliation language is used theologically is in the Second Book of Maccabees, where it appears in several passages for God's 'being reconciled' to the people (2 Macc. 1:5; 5:20; 7:33; 8:29).

The third distinctive aspect of reconciliation language is that it is also isolated within the New Testament literature to the Apostle Paul, and then in only a few passages (1 Cor. 7:11; Rom. 5:10–11; 11:15; 2 Cor. 5:18–20; Eph. 2:1–21). Although the actual terms seldom appear, the notion of reconciliation is nevertheless a central one for Paul, working itself out in the argument of Romans, 2 Corinthians and Ephesians.

Finally, reconciliation language is distinctive because of its inherently reciprocal character: relations between parties cannot fundamentally be altered unless both parties agree. This makes reconciliation, in contrast to 'salvation' or 'purification', an understanding of the mystery that is deeply 'relational' (in the contemporary sense of that term) – an invitation that requires a response. It also makes reconciliation language one that we can use for our relations with each other as well as with God.

Indeed, reconciliation has vaulted from an obscure place in the New Testament theological lexicon to a central position for many contemporary Christians. In the USA, churches that explicitly include homosexual members are called 'Reconciling Congregations'. In South Africa, under the influence of Archbishop Tutu, the period after Apartheid had been devoted to 'Truth and Reconciliation'. Many of the expressions for God's work among humans have become threadbare from overuse. Reconciliation seems fresh and powerful and particularly pertinent in a world that, even as it approaches becoming a global village, finds that humans find countless ways to divide themselves into hostile camps.

Precisely because it seems so pertinent and powerful to us, however, reconciliation can be quickly cheapened, as other theological jargon has been, through careless and excessive use. And if reconciliation is to remain a properly theological category, rather than simply a political ploy, then we must pay some attention to the way in which Paul speaks of reconciliation, not as something that humans can easily accomplish among themselves, but as something that humans can accomplish at all only because God has acted among them first.

To change a situation of alienation between parties, it is necessary for the parties to change. They must turn from attitudes of fear, suspicion, and hatred, to attitudes of confidence, trust, and love. Such change is difficult. Nations and neighbourhoods and families most often found it nearly impossible. One of the great 'mysteries of iniquity', in fact, is how the process of alienation, once begun, can scarcely be reversed. We have all, in congregations, communities, families, marriages, seen it happen or experienced the slow and deadly drift toward total non-communication, that perhaps began with the slightest of hurts or misundandings. Once parties have 'irreconcilable differences' (hate each other), the only option to mutual destruction seems to be complete avoidance or divorce. How can a bridge be built across a chasm that constantly grows wider?

RECONCILIATION WITH GOD THROUGH CHRIST

The remarkable aspect of Paul's understanding of reconciliation is that he turns the tables of expectation. In ordinary human circumstances, we would understand the one who has caused the alienation to be the one responsible for reconciling. This, in fact, is what Paul says about the wife who separates from her husband, not that he should reconcile with her, but that she should reconcile with him (1 Cor. 7:11). She is the agent of separation, she must be the agent of reconciliation. Paul understands that human beings have been the agents of alienation from God. Their sin has made them 'enemies' of God. But humans by themselves are not able to repair this rupture. If God and humans are to be at peace, then it is God who must bring it about. But God brings it about – and here it gets interesting – precisely through the human being Jesus! For Paul, Jesus represents both the offer and the acceptance of reconciliation between God and humans.

This is Paul's argument in his letter to the Romans, where his thesis concerns the way in which God has established humans in right relationship with himself through faith (Rom. 1:16–17). Paul begins by showing how humans have turned away from God through disobedience, withdrawing ever further from the source of their being and therefore ever further from the way of life that accords with God's image (Rom. 1:18–3:20). Then Paul shows how God has turned things around through the faithful death of Jesus (3:21–26). After arguing that 'righteousness through faith and not through law' was the basis of God's promise of life all along, as revealed in the story of Abraham (4:1–25), Paul returns in Romans 5 to the astonishing gift God has given. Through the faithful obedience of Jesus, humans have 'peace with God through our Lord Jesus Christ' (5:1). It is through him, Paul says, that 'we have obtained access to this gift in which we stand' (5:2).

Paul spells out the extraordinary character of the gift – and its cost – using the specific language of reconciliation:

> While we were still weak, at the right time Christ died for the ungodly. Why, one will hardly die for a righteous man – though perhaps for a good man one will dare even to die. But God shows his love for us in that while we were yet sinners, Christ died for us. Since, therefore, we are now justified by his blood, much more shall we be saved by him from the wrath of God. For if while we were enemies we were reconciled to God by the death of his son, much more, now that we are reconciled, shall we be saved by his life. Not only so, but we also rejoice in God through our Lord Jesus Christ, through whom we have now received our reconciliation.
>
> (Rom. 5:6–11)

Paul then spells out the nature of the faith through which we were reconciled to God by contrasting the disobedience of Adam – the start of humanity's tale of alienation – and the obedience of Jesus (5:12–21).

In this argument, Paul makes three critical points concerning reconciliation. First, it is costly, demanding in some circumstances even death. Second, it is not simply a matter of gestures, but also a matter of dispositions – it required Christ's obedient faith. Third, and most surprising, reconciliation demands that the strong become weak so that the weak can become strong: in the gift of God in Christ, we see that God reached across the barrier that humans had established. They were in the wrong. But they were also 'weak' and unable to cross over the gap of alienation.

God shows his love for us, Paul declares, in that while we were still sinners Christ died for us (5:8).

For Paul, those who receive gifts must share them. The gift of reconciliation from God, accomplished in Christ, is to be shared among the Roman faithful in their life together. When they dispute over matters of diet or the observance of special days, they are not 'to let what you eat cause the ruin of one for whom Christ died' (14:15). The pattern of Christ's reconciling death is to shape their community attitudes and actions. This demands more of the strong: 'We who are strong ought to bear with the failings of the weak, and not to please ourselves; let each of us please his neighbor for his good, to edify him. For Christ did not please himself; but, as it is written, "The reproaches of those who reproach thee fell on me" [Ps. 69:9] . . . welcome one another, therefore, as Christ has welcomed you, for the glory of God' (Rom 15:1–7).

RECONCILIATION IN REAL LIFE

The most dramatic language concerning reconciliation in the New Testament comes in Paul's second letter to the Corinthians. It is dramatic above all because it is forged in the context of real alienation between Paul and his beloved community.

Already in 1 Corinthians we catch hints that not all is well between this powerfully gifted but competitive community and its founder. Not only are the Corinthians fighting between themselves over matters of 'everyday life' (1 Cor. 6:3), and even going to pagan courts to settle their disputes about dietary and sexual matters (6:1–7), but they are not at all certain that Paul has any special authority to teach them. Some in the community prefer other teachers (1:10–11). In his first letter to them, then, Paul struggles to establish his own authority to teach (1–4) even as he tries to convert them from a competitive frame of mind to one of collaboration and mutual upbuilding, on the model of 'the mind of Christ' (2:16) revealed through Jesus's death on the cross (1:18–31). There, God had shown how God's weakness is stronger than human strength, God's foolishness wiser than human wisdom

(1:25). In his instructions to the Corinthians, Paul tried to apply that same pattern: even when someone was 'right', it was more important to be 'righteous', that is, be willing to forego one's 'rights' in order to strengthen the brothers and sisters for whom Christ died (8:7–13).

By the time Paul writes Second Corinthians, it is clear that things have got worse rather than better. Three things seem to have exacerbated the tension between the apostle and his church. The major problem is that Paul has invited the Corinthians to take part in his great collection for the church in Jerusalem (1 Cor. 16:1–4), but his way of managing the collection has made some among the Corinthians suspect that Paul and his delegates have been defrauding them (2 Cor. 11:7–11; 12:15–18). When among them, Paul had made a great claim of preaching for free (1 Cor. 9:12–18), but now when he is away, he sends representatives to pick up large funds – who knows where the money is really going? A second factor is that Paul has overstepped his authority in rebuking a member of the community, which has caused 'sorrow' among some (2 Cor. 2:1–11). These perceived abuses, in turn, have stimulated the Corinthians' interest in rival teachers (11: 1–6). Paul calls them 'superapostles' (11:5; 12:11) and claims that they 'peddle the word of God' (2:17), but in the eyes of the congregation, they at least are straightforward in their preaching for pay – a practice even Paul says is supported by nature, the law, and the command of Jesus (1 Cor. 9:7–14)!

Paul's situation is painful. He is engaged in what he considers his major project of reconciliation between Gentile and Jewish churches. He agreed with the leaders in Jerusalem to make this collection (Gal. 2:10), and the gesture has become more important because of the tensions that his mission to the Gentiles has created (Acts 21:20; Rom. 15:31). The gift of money symbolizes, in the logic of ancient friendship, a spiritual as well as a material sharing (Rom. 15:27; 2 Cor. 8:14). Paul has gone to extraordinary efforts, and has told the churches in Macedonia that the churches in Achaia had already reached their pledge (2 Cor. 9:1–2). Now, at the critical moment, the church that is his own signature, the letter of recommendation for his apostleship 'written by the spirit in the heart' (2 Cor. 3:3), has balked at participating because of its suspicion and dislike of its founder. Paul is in the awkward situation of seeking reconciliation with a church now alienated from him, so that the church will join in the great act of reconciliation among churches that are estranged.

One of the reasons 2 Corinthians is so difficult to read – some have even despaired of reading it as a single letter and think of it as a patched-up set of separate notes – is that Paul's rhetoric is shaped by such a complex and difficult situation. Three dimensions of his rhetoric are worth noting, as we think about how the divine mystery of reconciliation might be translated into relations between humans.

First, Paul seeks reconciliation with his church by speaking the truth, as he sees it, about their estrangement. He not only touches on the points that divide them (we would not know them if he had not!), he defends himself and expresses his hurt and anger at the state of affairs in which other apostles are being preferred to him. In chapters 10–12, he acknowledges that he is making himself 'weak' and 'foolish' by his boasting. But he does this in imitation of Christ's weakness and foolishness on the cross (2 Cor. 13:1–4). Paul must make the Corinthians see that by rejecting their apostle, they are rejecting the very basis on which they have been empowered by God. Whatever they think of him, they must acknowledge that through him, the power of God had been at work (12:11–13). Paul makes himself extraordinarily vulnerable. He could have turned away from them when they rejected him, and cultivated the Philippians, with whom he was always friends (Phil. 4:10–20). But he chooses to appear as foolish and weak, for their sake rather than his. Without the truth about the hurt that has been done, there cannot be reconciliation.

Second, Paul reminds the Corinthians that neither he nor they are the point, but rather the truth of the Gospel of Christ. It is not a matter of who's right, it is a matter of being rightly related together. Paul therefore summons them to the mission of reconciliation that was God's work in Christ:

If anyone is in Christ, he is a new creation; the old has passed away, behold, the new has come. All this is from God, who through Christ reconciled us to himself and gave us the ministry of reconciliation; that is, in Christ, God was reconciling the world to himself, not counting their trespasses against them, and entrusting to us the message of reconciliation. So we are ambassadors for Christ, God making his appeal through us. We beseech you on behalf of Christ, be reconciled to God.

(2 Cor. 5:17–20)

Paul sees God's work of reconciliation in Christ as an exchange. Christ died so that others might live (4:13–15). He became sin so that others might become righteous (5:21). He became poor so that others might become rich (8:9). Paul therefore sees the ministry of reconciliation as involving the same self-emptying for the sake of others. The apostle carries about the death of Jesus so that others might live (4:7–12). He makes himself foolish so that others might become wise with the mind of Christ (11: 16–12:13). Paul and the Corinthians are called, in short, to participate in a reality larger than their small hurts and misunderstandings; they are called to share in God's work of reconciliation in the world.

Third, Paul makes bold to summon his estranged readers to join in the great act of reconciliation that was his collection for the saints in Jerusalem (2 Cor. 8–9). He takes a great risk in doing so. They might refuse. But he takes a greater risk in not doing so, for the truth of the Gospel, and obedience to that truth, is at stake (2 Cor. 9:12–15). No matter that Paul and the Corinthians are in dispute. They are nevertheless called to God's work for the world. Paul understands, as well, that a way for estranged parties to find reconciliation is to join together in a great work for others, and in that shared work, to discover again the deep roots of their own relationship in Christ.

Although Second Corinthians is daunting in its language and its thought, the letter repays close and careful reading. In this impassioned letter, we find Paul at his most pastoral. He is pushed by the peril of his own circumstances to think deeply about the mystery of reconciliation, not only between God and humans, but also among humans who have been gifted by God in Christ. He took a great risk in making himself so vulnerable to his readers, showing his hurt and anger at the very moment he challenged them to obey the demand of the Gospel. Did Paul succeed? Did he find reconciliation with his estranged community? There are two indicators that he did. In his letter to the Romans, he mentions that the churches in Achaia also contributed to the collection (Rom. 15:26). And, we know, the Corinthians saved his letters.

Chapter 11

The Things that Make for Peace

A Reading of James 3:13–4:10

The title of this reflection on the Letter of James comes from the Gospel of Luke, which portrays Jesus as lamenting over Jerusalem immediately before entering the city to royal acclaim: 'If you had only recognized on this day,' he cries, 'the things that make for peace.' Because they were hidden from their eyes, he continues, they 'did not recognize the time of [their] visitation from God', and their experience of war and destruction was inevitable (Luke 19:41–44).

Christian rhetoric on war and peace tends to be ineffective for two obvious reasons. First, it responds to acute circumstances more than it does to chronic conditions. Threat of a military draft, or a proposed plan of attack, can mobilize preachers and marchers for peace. But quotidian patterns of aggression and violence fail to energize resistance. Second, even when attention is given to oppressive social systems and unjust economic practices as the deep roots of war, analysis remains superficial, because it does not deal with the seemingly intractable pathology that constantly renews such patterns.

Because we do not give close and consistent attention to 'the things that make for peace,' or, conversely, 'the things that make for war' everyday on playgrounds and street corners, our speech is rightly heard (even by ourselves) as belated and shallow when nations clash in battle.

Perhaps the same tendencies account for the lack of attention paid to the one New Testament text that actually asks the question concerning the source of war, 'From where do wars, and from where do battles among you come?' and, more remarkably, proposes an answer, 'Is it not from your desires that are at war among your members?' (James 4:1). The Letter of James proposes that human conflict and violence is directly connected to disordered and conflicted desires.

This does not, at first glance, seem terribly helpful for dealing with wars between nations. But the problem does not lie in James' statement. It lies rather in our short-attention span. We always press for a quick and simple answer, rather than the close examination of a question. The question concerning the source of battles and wars among us is always worth asking. And if we follow out the logic of James' argument, we discover a genuinely helpful way of thinking about violence on both the small and the great scale.

James' question and answer are placed within a call to conversion that extends from 3:13–4:10 and provides the basic framework for understanding this intensely dualistic moral exhortation. As everywhere in his composition, James seeks an integrity of profession and practice among his readers. His call is to those he calls the 'double-minded' (*dipsychoi*) in 1:8 and 4:8, those who want to claim 'the faith of our glorious Lord Jesus Christ' (2:1) but who also want to live in ways conformable, not to the measure of that faith, but to the measure of 'the world' (see 2:1–6).

This call to conversion has two parts, an indictment in 3:13–4:6, and a summons to repentance in 4:7–10. The rhetorical climax of the indictment is 4:4: 'You adulteresses! Do you not know that friendship with the world is enmity with God? Therefore, whoever chooses to be a friend of the world is established as an enemy of God.' By calling his readers 'adulteresses', James invokes the ancient prophetic metaphor of covenant as marriage: he suggests that his readers are promiscuous in loyalty, declaring that they are friends of God while seeking also to be friends of the world.

James' language about friendship has roots in Greek philosophy, which considered friendship the most serious of human commitments, one in which friends thought alike and shared all possessions in common. His point is that his 'double-minded' readers want to be friends with everyone. But if 'God' and 'world' stand as two opposing measures of truth, it is impossible to be friends with both. Even wanting to be a 'friend of the world' means to be established as an 'enemy of God.'

None of this language makes sense apart from a closer look at the terms of the indictment in 3:13–4:6 and the terms of the summons to conversion in 4:7–10. The first thing we notice is that the two parts correspond in many of their terms: the 'purifying of the heart' in 4:8 matches the 'selfish ambition of the heart' in 3:14, as well as the 'purity' of the wisdom in 3:17; the 'dejection' of 4:9 corresponds to the 'arrogance' of 4:6; the 'double-minded' of 4:8 is the opposite of the 'undivided' in 3:17. Most obviously, the final command and promise, 'humble yourselves before God and he will exalt you' (4:10) picks up from the 'lowly' of 4:6 as well as the pattern of the wisdom 'from below/from above' in 3:13–17. The entire passage is set up in terms of an opposition between two ways of living in the world. One is according to a wisdom that is 'earthbound, unspiritual, demonic', the other is according to a wisdom that is 'from above', and is 'peaceable, gentle, open to persuasion, filled with mercy and good fruits' (3:15–17). James insists that one cannot be 'friends' with both views of reality. One must choose.

Placing James' statement about the source of war in the context of his call to conversion from one form of wisdom to another, we can look more closely at his discussion in terms pertinent to war and peace. Peace-seekers always look first for an expression of the ideal, and James provides a wonderful positive statement: 'The fruit of righteousness is sown in peace by the makers of peace' (3:18). As so often in James, we can hear in this declaration echoes of the Matthean beatitudes: 'Blessed are those who hunger and thirst for righteousness, for they will be filled . . . blessed are the peacemakers for they shall be called children of

God' (Matt. 5:6–9). But James offers the serious seeker after peace something far more: an analysis of those things that 'do not make for peace'.

Notice that in his short indictment, James speaks of 'bitter jealousy' in 3:14, 'jealousy and selfish ambition' in 3:16, 'you are jealous' in 4:2, and climactically in 4:5, 'does the Scripture speak in vain? Does the spirit he made to dwell in us crave enviously?' All of these references to envy are connected to the 'wisdom from below' that 'boasts and lies against the truth' (3:14), and which expresses itself in 'disorder and every mean practice' (3:16). James links envy and social unrest. It is against this backdrop that we must read the difficult set of statements in 4:2. Immediately after declaring that wars and battles stem from the desires that are at war in our members, James says: 'you desire and you do not have: so you kill. You are jealous and cannot obtain: so you battle and wage war.' James seems to say that envy lies at the root of social disorder, violence, murder and war.

For ancient readers, James's associations would have been neither new nor surprising, for Graeco-Roman philosophy had long given careful attention to the vice of envy, and had consistently connected envy to social unrest, murder, and war. In many ways, envy was considered to be the opposite of friendship. If friendship tended toward the sharing of all things and harmony between persons, envy was regarded as the most disruptive of vices. Ancients regarded envy as the most ignoble vice. Graeco-Roman moralists thought of virtue in terms of health and vice in terms of sickness. The status of envy can be gathered from Socrates' designation of it as 'the ulcer of the soul.' Aristotle defined envy as a certain sorrow that someone experiences because someone has something. But why should another's possession cause me sorrow? And why in these ancient discussions is envy so consistently considered the cause of social upheaval and war?

To understand this, we need to move a little deeper into the logic of envy. It is based on the premise that being is a matter of having. Greater being (and worth and power) is a function of greater having (of whatever sort of possessions). To have more is to be more. Now, in a closed system, in a world defined in terms of finite resources, there is a limited amount of 'having' available, and for one to be 'more' means inevitably that another is 'less'. This is the world of quantitative measurement, of comparison, of competition. Envy expresses itself as 'sorrow' because I experience grief when you have more than me. Why? Because I am necessarily diminished by your having more than me. Envy flourishes particularly among 'near-equals' who compete on the same plane. Thus the proverb going all the way back to Hesiod: 'Potter envies potter.'

The grief and rage of envy at one's perceived loss and diminishment because of the success of another turns active in the form of arrogance (*hyperēphania*), which the ancients again consistently associate with envy, as does James as well (4:6). Arrogance 'boasts and lies against the truth' (3:14), not because it is strong, but because it is weak. Arrogance is not the opposite of envy, as we might at first think, but its active expression. Arrogance seeks to dominate others, to seize their possessions, precisely because of the terror of non-being connected to *not* having the most possessions, or the possessions that are thought (at our particular potters' bench) to seem the most worth having, if we are to have real being and worth. Envy turns aggressive through arrogance.

Once we grasp the basic logic of envy, we can grasp as well the profound insight of the ancients into the roots not only of war, but of all competition that leads to violence and social unrest: 'you desire and you do not have: so you kill. You are jealous and cannot obtain: so you do battle and wage war' (James 4:2). And we can see that this analysis applies not only to nations in armed conflict over real or perceived possessions (whether oil or land or 'honour'), but as well to children killing each other in schoolyards over the best brand of running shoes ('to be is to own Nike').

Even more important, we can see that the logic of envy is at work pervasively in the competitive character of our culture, not least in the form of an economic system that has as its premise precisely the equation between having more and being worth more. Competition is at the heart of capitalism. And commerical advertising fashions its rhetoric precisely to appeal to the envy within every fearful human heart that is terrified at its lack of real being and real worth, and is easily convinced that being and worth can be purchased, or otherwise acquired.

The irony that James employs in this passage is intense. Friend-ship in antiquity, as I suggested, was all about commonality, sharing spiritually as well as materially. When James says that his readers' attitudes of envy and arrogance make them 'friends of the world', he is deliberately mixing what in antiquity should not have been mixed. To be 'friends of the world' was to think and act precisely according to the logic of envy, and therefore, in one fashion or another, to be in fundamental competition with other humans, and, at some level or other, seeking their elimination. The other parts of the letter show what this logic looks like. It is operative in the rich who oppress the poor legally by suing them in courts (2:6) and illegally by withholding the wages of the day-laborers in the field (5:1–6). It is at work in the arrogance of the businessmen who assume the future and reduce everything to a matter of gain (4:13–16).

The logic is also found to be at work, however, among those who claim to be 'friends of God', yet live their lives as though defined by the same premises of envy and arrogance, only in a 'double-minded' fashion: those who claim the 'faith of Jesus Christ', yet scorn the poor man in the assembly while catering to the rich (2:1–5); those who tell the naked and starving 'go in peace' without providing what they need to get through the day (2:14–17); those who bless God and then turn about and curse those created in the image of God (3:9); those who exercise the secret arrogance of slandering their neighbor in order to elevate themselves (4:11).

All these patterns are 'the things that make for war', and, says James, God stands against them. Quoting Proverbs 3:34, James says flatly: 'God resists the arrogant' (4:6). And after describing those who oppress the poor through withholding their wages, James says: 'You have condemned, you have murdered the righteous one. Does He not oppose you?' (5:6). James' call to conversion intends to turn those who are double-minded, who want to be friends with the world as well as God, to singleness of devotion: 'purify your hearts, you double-minded!' (4:8). Such conversion demands precisely the opposite of the self-exaltation and arrogance that are driven by envy: 'submit therefore to God . . . humble yourselves before the Lord and he will exalt you' (4:7, 10).

In order truly to do 'the things that make for peace', however, it is necessary to be 'friends with God' in a single-minded fashion rather than double-mindedly. Following the understanding assumed by James, this means seeing the world from God's own perspective and acting in accordance with that 'wisdom from above'. What is this understanding of reality? The opposite of the logic of envy, which views the world as a closed system of limited resources for which all are in competition. James calls his readers to see the world rather as one drenched constantly with God's gifts. God is the one who 'gives more grace' to the lowly (4:6). God is the one who 'gives to all simply and without grudging' (1:5), and 'every good giving and every perfect gift is from above, coming down from the father of lights. With him there is no alteration of shadow of change' (1:17). Rather than a closed system in which humans must fight for position, the world is constantly renewed by the constantly renewed gift of existence, life, and worth, from the one who 'by his decision, gave us birth through a word of truth, in order that we might be a kind of first-fruits of his creatures' (1:18).

To be wholeheartedly 'friends of God', then, means to be generous and constant sharers of the goods of creation, knowing that having does not in the least add to our being or worth, and that the logic of gift-giving is to share the gifts given us. Such a view of reality generates a logic of friendship with others rather than of competition, a spirit of collaboration and cooperation rather than one of competition. It means receiving the poor man in the assembly with more honour than the rich man, because the poor have been promised the kingdom (2:5). It means clothing and feeding the naked and hungry, because 'judgement is without mercy to the merciless, but mercy overcomes even judgement' (2:13). It means, like Abraham, that 'friend of God' (2:23), being willing to give up even the precious gift of life from God. It means, like Rahab, to welcome strangers as messengers of God (2:26). It means speaking the truth simply (5:12), gathering around the weak to support them (5:13–15), confessing sins each to the other (5:16) and offering mutual correction to those who stray from the path of truth (5:19–20). Such patterns of behaviour form the 'fruit of righteousness sown in peace by the makers of peace' (3:18), not in spectacular or even visible fashion, but in the quiet, 'pure, peaceable, gentle, open to persuasion' manner of life that reveals the wisdom from above, 'filled with mercy and all good fruits', by people who are 'not divided, not insincere' (3:17).

James 3:13–4:10 is a call to conversion. It challenges each reader to consider the ways in which friendship with God is compromised by a friendship with the world that leads to strife and war. It demands of us careful consideration not only of James' words but also the patterns of our everyday life. It reminds us that the things that make for peace may be simple but they are never easy.

Part Two:

Scripture

Chapter 12

Renewing Catholic Biblical Scholarship

A call for the renewal of Catholic biblical scholarship in 2001 may strike some as odd. Isn't that exactly what has been happening over the past 60 years since Pope Pius XII, in his encyclical, *Divini Afflante Spiritu*, opened the way for Catholic scholars to approach the Bible with the same historical-critical methods long employed by Protestant scholars? Well, yes and no. From some perspectives, biblical scholarship looks robust, indeed. There are more people with advanced degrees in biblical studies producing more scholarship than ever before. There's lots of product. From another perspective, precisely all that activity and production appears as a problem. Is there any point to it all? I am among a small number who see a crisis in biblical scholarship generally. It is increasingly removed from the life of the Church sociologically: the academic rather than the faith community is its context. And it is less and less connected to the questions important to the Church: biblical scholars increasingly are historians rather than theologians. And if there is a crisis for biblical scholarship generally, there is a crisis in particular for Catholic biblical scholarship, for the story of the last 60 years has been partly about Catholics finding their way into exciting new territory, and partly about losing a sense of where they are from and where they are going. A call for renewal therefore is not a call for learning new things but for remembering some older things that we ought not to have forgotten.

THE OLD COUNTRY

Perhaps it would be useful to remember that Catholics did interpret the Bible before 1943, and had been doing so for some 1900
years! To see the changes for good and bad over the past few
years, we can begin by reminding ourselves of the characteristics,
good and bad, of Scripture scholarship within the church in
that lengthy early period. The good side is that the study of
Scripture and Catholic tradition existed in harmonious relationship. Scripture was not something separate from liturgy and
the life of faith. Catholics did not study Scripture as a subject.
They learned it (more than they usually suspected!) within and
from the practices of piety. The liturgy, both the Eucharist and
the divine office, are scriptural through and through. Catholics
could imagine the world imagined by Scripture because that
world was constructed constantly through the practices of faith.
This ground-level experience of Scripture, in turn, was nourished
by a long scholarly conversation about Scripture that extended
from the earliest bishops and martyrs through the monks and
mendicants down to the clergy of the local parish. Several strong
convictions ran through this long conversation: that Scripture is
God's inspired word, that it is life-giving and transforming, that it
speaks in many ways and at many levels – not only as a historical
witness to the past, but as a prophetic witness to the present life of
faith. Such interpretation of Scripture took place entirely within
and for the life of the Church. Scholars were priests and religious
who learned Scripture as part of theology, who preached at Mass,
who could not have conceived of a mode of scriptural interpretation that was simply about knowledge rather than about
edification.

There was also a bad side to the state of Catholic biblical
scholarship before 1943. Yes, it was in living conversation with
tradition, but too often, the conversation was one-sided: the
witness of Scripture could be swallowed up by tradition, so that it
only confirmed and never challenged the Church's practices. Yes,
the reading of Scripture at several levels enriched the imagination,

but a neglect of the literal sense sometimes led to fantasies only loosely attached to Scripture itself. Yes, a lively and imaginative engagement with Scripture extended through the centuries, but it was carried out in contexts and languages unavailable to most Catholics: the riches of the divine office were in Latin and accessible mainly to monks, the riches of the Mass were also in Latin and unintelligible to most laypeople. Yes, Scripture and theology went together in the training and practice of the clergy, but this meant the exclusion of laypeople and in particular women from active participation in scriptural interpretation.

Pope Pius XII's encyclical affirmed all the traditional values in Catholic scriptural interpretation, but it also enabled scholars to practise the historical method that had dominated biblical scholarship among Protestants for over a hundred years. Included in this opening was an encouragement to seek the original sense of and to translate into modern languages the original Hebrew and Greek in addition to the Latin Vulgate. Small wonder that scholars as well as the ordinary faithful considered the Pope's letter a cause for unalloyed joy and hope. At the simplest level, it allowed scholars the same freedom of inquiry that was enjoyed by Protestant colleagues but that had formerly been forbidden them. The move into historical study seemed also to encourage ecumenism: Catholics now joined a wider conversation, and one in which all participants shared the same objective methods; how could greater understanding and agreement among denominations not follow as a result? Translation from Hebrew and Greek into modern languages meant also the production of research and teaching instruments geared to this new knowledge, so that the circle of participation within the Catholic community could be enlarged to include laity as well as clergy. Finally, there could be hope that, just as historical study was renewing the liturgy, so could the historical approach within biblical studies enable a similar renewal of scriptural study and appreciation among Catholics.

BRAVE NEW WORLD?

After 60 years, the brave new world of historical-critical biblical scholarship has turned out to be more ambiguous than anticipated. Not all Catholic scholars yet see things this way. Some of my colleagues think things are just fine. It depends a bit on one's generation and one's personal experience. I speak as a Catholic New Testament scholar born in 1943 (the year of Pius XII's encyclical), who was nurtured by the rich traditions of the liturgy and the divine office as a teenage seminarian and then as a Benedictine monk. Leaving the monastery, I did doctoral work in New Testament at Yale – a bastion of the historical critical approach – and have taught in both Protestant seminaries at Yale and Emory, as well as in a state university, for the past 35 years. I belong to what might be called the 'third generation' of Catholic scholars following *Divini Afflante Spiritu*.

Like my earlier use of the phrases 'new territory', and 'brave new world', my reference to 'generations' evokes the classic experience of North American immigrants. Sociological studies show that first, second and third generation immigrants to the United States from a European country characteristically had different perceptions because of their distinct experiences. I am suggesting that 'historical-critical scholarship' represented an analogous 'new world' experience for Catholic biblical scholars.

First generation immigrants to America (say, from Italy) were so Italian in language and culture that, in some sense, 'becoming American' simply meant being Italian in a new place, but with new citizenship rights and new opportunities. Similarly, the first generation of Catholic scholars who engaged historical-critical methods were so thoroughly Catholic in their training and sensibility that the new methods simply represented an enrichment rather than a replacement. Second generation immigrants to America, however, often want to forget 'the old country' entirely. They want to be more American than the Americans. They resent the Italian the parents still speak at home; they learn how to 'pass' so that no one would ever guess that they were

Italian. In the same fashion, second-generation Catholic biblical scholars sought total assimilation into the new world that had been dominated by Protestant scholars. They wanted to play the historical game even better than the natives. And if the game is essentially an academic one, then they would write larger commentaries with more footnotes, to prove they belonged.

Third generation immigrants typically sense that they have lost as much as they have gained by their complete assimilation into American culture. They are now unequivocally like everyone else, but what use is that? They certainly do not want to return to Italy, and probably don't want to learn Italian, but they seek some sense of roots; perhaps learning to cook lasagne as Grandma used to make it would be a start. In the same way, biblical scholars of my (third) generation are becoming aware that the complete assimilation of Catholics into the guild of scholarship has been a mixed blessing. Yes, Catholics now are recognized as leaders in the field; yes, Catholics are found in the best university positions; yes, Catholics head various academic journals and societies. But in what sense are they still Catholic? My generation of Catholic Scripture scholars is (or ought be be) going through a period of self-examination concerning the state of biblical scholarship and what it means to be a Catholic engaged in this ever-growing academic field. Although it is well aware of and appreciates the gains made by the previous two generations, and although it certainly does not want to return to 'the old country' in which the Vulgate was the required text and historical criticism was forbidden, my generation nevertheless asks whether some of the gains have been too expensive, whether as much has been lost as gained, whether there are some values from 'the old country' that we need to look at more closely.

On close examination of hard experience, for example, it seems clear that the historical-critical approach is deeply deficient, especially when it is the sole way of reading Scripture. To be sure, the more history we learn, the more intelligible the texts of the Bible become, and the more responsible we can be in our analogous reasoning on the basis of the Bible. But the historical-critical approach has never been content with learning history in order to better hear Scripture. It has been far more preoccupied with historical reconstruction with the use of biblical sources, whether of ancient Israel, the early church, or most notoriously, the 'historical Jesus.' The very efforts to carry out such reconstructions have revealed the limitations of the enterprise. Catholics reasonably wonder why self-designated objective scholars using purportedly objective methods on identical sources should end up with such widely divergent results. More significantly, the historical approach has as its entire purpose keeping Scripture in the past. Ostensibly, this is so we can encounter its otherness and challenge. In fact, however, the historical chase is often its own reward, and the ability of the historical approach to inform theology or nurture faith has not been decisively demonstrated.

Some Catholic scholars' disenchantment with the historical-critical approach is accompanied by a growing awareness that by no means has this approach been truly objective or neutral. The 'new land' that Catholics entered after Pius XII was one in which implicitly protestant theological presuppositions governed the populace and its practices. If the spirit of Catholicism can be termed an attitude of 'both/and', the spirit of Protestantism (especially in the form of the Lutheranism that shaped the historical-critical approach) can be called an attitude of 'either/ or.' Thus, biblical scholarship tends to adopt the posture of the reformation that pitted Scripture against tradition: the recovery of scriptural origins was meant precisely to challenge the developed doctrine and practice of the Church. In the Enlightenment secularization of this reformation impulse, the either/or was more radical, taking the form of reason against Scripture. The point of the scholar became to critically assess the shape and substance of Scripture itself, as though from a superior vantage point, rather than humbly seeking to discover its ways. In the American institutionalization of this spirit, we find the secular university not only separate from but actively antagonistic toward the Church.

The either/or is expressed also by opposing Christian origins to the development of the church. The preoccupation with the 'apostolic age' and the dismissal of the second century as a decline in the direction of 'Early Catholicism' has nothing to do with sober historiography and everything to do with theological commitments that are specifically Protestant in character. In this view, even the earliest development of the Church was already a corruption of its original spirit, and historical study serves the cause of reformation by its recovery of pristine origins. The pure form of this commitment is the preference for the 'historical Jesus' to 'the Christ of Faith', as though even the Gospels got Jesus wrong. While Catholics have always looked to the apostolic age as a norm for its authentic life (witness the reform movements of monks and mendicants), it has considered development less as corruption – although that too has happened – than as a spirit-guided discernment through time of how to adapt the apostolic witness to new circumstances. And while Catholics look to the humanity of Jesus as the measure of their identity, they find that humanity perfectly portrayed in the literary representations of the Gospels rather than in the cardboard reconstructions of historians.

The either/or expresses itself also in the opposition between the literal sense of the text and the figurative. The reformation began by insisting that only the literal sense of Scripture could guide the life of the church, whereas all forms of allegory were dangerous distractions. The historical-critical approach has pushed that opposition relentlessly, to such an extent that even the allegorical interpretations of the parables offered by the Gospels themselves are considered less authentic and less worthy of Jesus. The insistence that the text must be read only in its historical context and can have only one historical meaning can become an implicit assertion that the Bible has only human authors and not a divine author, that its lessons therefore can only be human lessons rather than divine instruction, that its depictions are locked in the past and cannot speak authoritatively to the present. Catholics have never considered the literal sense of Scripture unimportant.

But because they have regarded Scripture as divinely inspired, they have appreciated the many ways in which Scripture can enlarge wisdom through the play of imagination.

The third generation of Catholic biblical scholars recognizes the sad paradox that although Catholic scholars are now universally recognized as full members of the critical guild, there is nothing recognizably Catholic in their scholarship. The tendencies within critical biblical scholarship drawing it away from the care and concern for the Church will in all probability only increase, as the centre of such scholarship – and above all the training of future seminary professors – increasingly becomes the secular university. Catholic scholars located in the most prestigious institutions of higher learning produce impressive volumes that are read by other scholars. Fewer and fewer of these leading biblical scholars can be called theologians in any sense; fewer and fewer of them write directly for lay readers among the faithful. If the older scholarship was a closed club because it allowed only male clergy, the newer scholarship threatens to become equally closed, not because it has failed to include lay and women participants, but because its scholarship is in service only to the small and specialized world of the academy rather than to the larger arena of the church in the public forum.

FORWARD NOT BACKWARD

The recovery of an authentically Catholic scriptural scholarship is urgent, for we are already well down the road of forgetfulness. We must begin now while a few of us remember some threads of continuity. But the way forward, I insist, must not be a turning backward. The Enlightenment has been, on the whole, a great benefit for humanity. The uses of history are many and important. By no means am I suggesting an obscurantist return to the situation before Pius XII. We could not return to pre-modernity even if we tried. We must rather enter into a stance that many now call 'post-modern,' which enables us to learn both from modernity and pre-modernity without being fully defined by either.

If we continue to affirm the central importance of history in biblical studies, for example, we must be willing to make some distinctions. We can affirm the need to learn history in order to understand the text, without agreeing that we should deconstruct the text in order to reconstruct history. We can acknowledge the use of history to decipher the original voice of the text, without agreeing that the original meaning is the only level of significance. We can recognize the critical functions of history, without limiting criticism to a single way of knowing (like the historical) but rather expanding it to include literary criticism, moral criticism and theological criticism of the text.

Then we must work together to restore something of the Catholic spirit of 'both/and' to biblical studies. This means first a concern not only for the time of origins but also the stages of development: Scripture as a living voice within the Church continued to speak and to be received in diverse ways that are significant not only for our understanding of our own history but also for our sense of the text's potential for meaning. Second, it means a commitment to the life of the Church, its living tradition. Catholic Scripture scholars bear a responsibility to bring their critical thinking to the contemporary Church as well as ancient texts. They must dare to be theologians. They must be brave enough to risk relevance. They must seek to build the Church and not only the academy. Third, Scripture scholars must dedicate themselves to the pedagogy that will begin to create genuine levels of biblical literacy among the laity and clergy alike. The Scripture scholar should not only ask how such ecclesial practices as decision-making are addressed by Scripture, but must also seek to construct practices that enable the Church to read Scripture together as Church.

Finally, contemporary Catholic scholars need to rejoin the longer conversation concerning the meanings of Scripture that extends from the second to the sixteenth century. Engaging this history of interpretation not only serves to illumine the text of Scripture, it can remind contemporary readers of certain sensibilities proper to those who are scholars in and for the Church.

One is the conviction that the inspired text speaks God's word as well as human words, and that the task of interpretation is essentially to seek the divine as well as or even more than the human word. Another is the openness to Scripture's speaking in many ways and at many different levels, able to feed the imaginative as well as the analytic mind. Another is that Scriptural interpretation is more than a matter of knowledge (*scientia*); it is also a matter of wisdom (*sapientia*), so that the scholar's work cannot stop short at explanation, it must seek transformation. Another is that it is possible to exercise the mind freely and critically without losing loyalty and love, that indeed the highest loyalty demands criticism, just as criticism demands the deepest loyalty.

All Catholics have a stake in the renewal of biblical scholarship. The Church cannot look to the academy for solutions, for the academy has problems enough of its own. Instead, the Church must begin to look to its own resources, seeking first to provide encouragement for the development of real practices of reading for transformation within the Church, and then demanding of its scholars that they learn to teach in a manner that builds the Church in love.

Chapter 13

The Holy Spirit in the New Testament

Writing about 'the Holy Spirit in the New Testament' is a more complex undertaking than it might at first appear. If we were to look at those places where the actual designation 'Holy Spirit' (*to pneuma to hagion*) appears, for example, we would indeed find such references in 15 of the 27 New Testament compositions, but would miss all of the language about 'spirit' that might also be pertinent, whether that term occurs alone, or is accompanied by modifiers such as 'the Spirit of the Lord' (2 Cor. 3:17), or 'the Spirit of God' (2 Cor. 3:3) or 'the Spirit of Christ' (1 Pet. 1:11), or 'spirit of sanctification' (Rom. 1:4), or 'spirit of prophecy' (Rev. 19:10), or 'Spirit of Jesus Christ' (Phil. 1:19). The fact that I am not certain which of these substantives to capitalize points to the problem: is all this talk of spirit about that whom Christians refer to as the Holy Spirit? This question, in turn, leads to the realization that the designation 'the Holy Spirit' as a person of the Holy Trinity does not come at the beginning of the Christian religion, but only after a long period of theological development that tried precisely to make sense of all these disparate sorts of statements about 'the Spirit' in the New Testament.

Our proper approach, then, is to return to the beginning point, to see how language about spirit works in these normative texts of our tradition. So pervasive and so complex is this language that we cannot hope to do it justice in a short chapter. But perhaps we can show enough of the power of this primordial symbol to suggest why authentic Christian 'spirituality' is to be defined as 'in the Holy Spirit'.

I use the word 'symbol' advisedly, as a reminder that, whereas what we speak of is certainly *real*, it is not the kind of reality that can be located in time and space, or defined physically, or pinned down historically, which means that our language, which works best with such definite things, must remain tentative and circumspect. The very word 'person' (*prosōpon*), which was hit upon by the patristic authors who hammered out the trinitarian doctrine, meant something quite different than what we intend by it, namely a specific and individual centre of consciousness inhabiting a human body. Indeed, we can only begin to approach that patristic sense of 'person' by observing the diverse functions assigned to this Holy Spirit in the New Testament writings. The 'Holy Spirit' begins to move from empty cipher to rich symbol as we learn of its activities and attributes.

VAGUE TERM

It may be useful to begin, however, with some attention to the expression itself. In the present-day Westernized world, few terms seem as vague and weak as the term 'spirit'. A large part of contemporary culture, indeed, works hard to deny the reality of spirit. We are the heirs of the great materialist explainers of the human drama: Darwin, Marx, Freud. Biologism rules. It is hard these days to get serious thinkers to admit to the possibility of 'mind', much less the reality of 'soul'. Concern for spirit and soul is the province of parapsychics and cultivators of the self. The dismissal of spirit, it seems, is a corollary of the denial of God. Serious people know that the realm of ghost stories is by definition not the real world, even, or perhaps especially, if the ghost is the 'Holy Ghost'.

What immediately becomes clear from the reading of the New Testament, in contrast, is the overwhelming *reality* of this Spirit. This is not, I think, simply a matter of the ancient Mediterranean world being more attuned to the existence of spiritual realms in general than we are, although that is also true. It is more a matter of the *experiential* basis for the Christian conviction concerning the Holy Spirit. The writers of the New Testament and the people for whom they wrote, in other words, did not reach the concept of the Holy Spirit by means of logical deduction or theological argument, but rather they attached the symbol 'Holy Spirit' to a certain set of experiences they claimed to be having.

These experiences, or what we can deduce about them, give us some insight into the meaning of the designation 'Holy Spirit'. The Christians claimed that they had been engaged not by a military or economic or physical power, but by something that affected them in *their* spirit, that is, in their human capacities for knowing and loving, in their freedom. They had been touched by a sort of power, an energy field, if you will, that was transformative, that enabled them to be, and speak, and act, in ways they had not previously known. The term 'spirit', then, designates the kind of experience they were claiming. Equally important, however, they claimed that their experience was not self-generated as a result of mass hysteria or self-hypnosis; it was not simply an adjustment within their *own* 'spirits'. The designation 'holy' signifies, as always in the biblical tradition, that the power thus encountered did not come from themselves, but from another, in this case 'the Other' who is God. Holiness is an attribute of God, who is 'different' from the world. Virtually without exception, language about the Holy Spirit in the New Testament can be taken as a symbol for the experience of the power and presence of God by humans. It is the symbol for the touch of contact between the divine and human spirit.

EXPERIENCE OF POWER

It is a touch, first of all, that is *powerful*. A close analysis of the claims of the first Christians concerning what had happened to them – that they were saved or freed, that they had bold access to God, that they were filled with joy, that they had newness of life – reveals these claims all involve an experience of power. And, to a remarkable extent, statements about power are also statements about the Holy Spirit. Thus, the difference between the ministries of Jesus and John in the Synoptic Gospels is stated simply: 'I have baptized you with water, but he will baptise you with the Holy Spirit' (Mark 1:8); Matthew and Luke add, 'and with fire' (Matt. 3:11; Luke 3:16). The commissioning of Jesus' followers in Luke 24:47–49 is described as Jesus sending 'the promise of the Father upon you . . . clothed with power from on high'. In fact, Luke has Jesus himself repeat that John's baptism was with water, but his witnesses 'will be baptized with the Holy Spirit' (Acts 1:5), a prophecy that is fulfilled at Pentecost, when the Holy Spirit fills the community with the power of prophetic utterance (Acts 2:1–13). Likewise the sending of the disciples in John's Gospel involves an empowerment by the Holy Spirit: 'he breathed on them and said to them, "Receive the Holy Spirit. If you forgive the sins of any, they are forgiven; if you retain the sins of any, they are retained" ' (John 20:20–23).

According to Acts 2:38, such empowerment by the Holy Spirit also came to believers when they were received into the messianic community by baptism: 'Repent, every one of you, in the name of Jesus Christ for the forgiveness of your sins, and you shall receive the gift of the Holy Spirit' (see also Matt. 28:19). This same Holy Spirit is the one who worked powerful deeds among believers (Gal. 3:3–5), empowering them to proclaim – 'And when they had prayed, the place where they were gathered together was shaken; and they were all filled with the Holy Spirit and spoke the word with boldness' (Acts 4:31; see 1 Thess. 1:5; 2 Tim. 1:6) – and even to profess their faith: 'No one speaking by the Spirit says, "Jesus be cursed", and no one can say, "Jesus is Lord", except by the Holy Spirit' (1 Cor. 12:3). And it is this Holy Spirit that enables the working of diverse ministries in the Church: 'all these are inspired by the one and the same Spirit, who apportions to each one individually as he wills' (1 Cor. 12:11). All of this talk of the Spirit was not about a wished-for ideal, but about a present and experienced reality. The Kingdom of God, Paul says, 'does not consist in talk but in power' (1 Cor. 4:20), and in Romans 15:20 he draws the connection explicitly: 'by the power of the Holy Spirit you may abound in hope'.

PERSONAL TOUCH

It is a touch, second, that is also *personal*. The language of power suggests energy and life, and it is above all with reference to the 'new life' of the resurrected Jesus that this symbol is connected. The resurrected Jesus promises the gift of the Holy Spirit to his followers. And at Pentecost, Peter proclaims: 'This Jesus, God raised up, and of that we are all witnesses. Being therefore exalted at the right hand of God, and having received from the Father the promise of the Holy Spirit, he has poured out this which you hear and see' (Acts 2:32–33). Please note the connection between the *experience of power*, the *gift of the Holy Spirit*, and the *resurrection of Jesus*. Peter says, '*he* has poured out', referring to Jesus.

The Holy Spirit is personal, then, in the sense that it derives from a living person, the risen Lord Jesus. But at this point, the New Testament texts present complications, for other texts speak of the Father sending the Spirit: 'Because you are sons, God has sent the spirit of his son into our hearts, crying, "Abba, Father" ' (Gal. 4:6). Precisely this ambiguity was at the heart of the rift between Catholic and Orthodox believers in the *filioque* controversy: did the Holy Spirit come from the Father *through* the Son (as the Orthodox insisted), or from the Father *and* the Son (as the Catholics insisted)? In fact, the New Testament says both things, which leaves us free to assert that the Holy Spirit comes from God and is the Spirit of Christ Jesus. Nowhere is this more dramatically stated than by Paul: 'the first Adam became a living being, the last Adam became a life-giving Spirit' (1 Cor. 15:45).

And because the Holy Spirit touches the human spirit with the power of the risen Christ, it is also *transformative*. The work of the Spirit is not simply to empower with extraordinary gifts the deed and speech, but above all to change the consciousness of believers in accordance with the pattern of the Messiah Jesus. The transformative work of the Holy Spirit is stated emphatically in 2 Corinthians 3:17–18: 'Now the Lord is the Spirit, and where the Spirit of the Lord is, there is freedom. And we all, with unveiled faces, beholding the glory of the Lord, are being changed into his likeness from one degree of glory into another; for this comes from the Lord, who is Spirit.'

Paul also says in Galatians 5:25: 'If we live by the Spirit, let us also walk by the Spirit.' In other words, the principle of new life among Christians is also to lead them into a new pattern of behaviour. Paul then spells out what this means: 'Bear one another's burdens, and so fulfil the law of Christ (*nomos tou christou*)' (Gal. 6:2). The phrase *nomos tou christou* might better be rendered 'the pattern of the Messiah', for Paul clearly means that the Holy Spirit is to transform us into the likeness of Jesus.

It is obvious that we cannot be changed into the physical likeness of the earthly Jesus; his Jewishness, his maleness, his language, these are all left in the unrecoverable past. But the Spirit who worked through Jesus can lead believers into the *pattern* of his life, that is, the character of Jesus' human obedience to God and service to others. Thus, in 1 Corinthians 2:12, Paul tries to show his readers how they should view reality in the light of the fact that 'we have received not the spirit of the world, but the spirit which is from God', and he closes this discussion with the flat statement 'we have the mind of Christ (*nous christou*)' (1 Cor. 2:16).

TRANSFORMATIVE

It is into this 'mind of Christ' that the Holy Spirit seeks to transform human consciousness and behaviour. Notice also, in Philippians 2:1–4, Paul says that if there is any 'participation in the Spirit', then his readers should 'do nothing from selfishness and conceit, but in humility count others better than yourself. Let each of you look not only to his own interests, but also to the interests of others.' He goes on, 'Have this mind among yourselves, which is yours in Christ Jesus', and continues with the Christ-hymn that describes Jesus in terms of his humbling himself and becoming obedient unto death (Phil. 2:5–11). For Paul, the transforming work of the Spirit is, as he speaks in his own person, 'that I may know him and the power of his resurrection, and may share his sufferings, becoming like him in his death, that if possible I might attain resurrection from the dead' (Phil. 3:10–11).

Some charismatic Christians are so caught up in the experience of the Spirit in its obvious and spectacular forms, such as speaking in tongues and prophecy and healing, that they tend to focus on these manifestations as though they were the final goal of the Spirit's work. They resist the painful necessity of transformation in the Spirit. This transformation is one by which God carves out a space for God's own freedom in our hearts, and it is inevitably painful. We move through the suffering of obedience and the humility of service towards the hope of a blessed resurrection. But if this transformation is resisted, then spirituality remains immature. The initial experience of excitement is sought over and over again addictively through the initiation of others into the same experience.

Certainly the gifts of the Holy Spirit – gifts of knowledge and speech and deed – are to be celebrated within the community of faith and accepted in thanksgiving. But in communities where such gifts are active, care must be taken to avoid an obsessive preoccupation with them, and with the sort of élitism toward which they can so easily move. Paul's discussion of the gifts in 1 Corinthians 12–14 should be mandatory and regular reading in such communities, with special attention to his insistence that the value of gifts lies in their usefulness to the building up of the community, so that it is often the quiet and ordinary gifts of service that should be valued above the noisy and spectacular gifts of speech.

Whether charismatic or not, however, all Christians should remember that the most fundamental work of the Spirit is to shape us into the image of Christ. Nowhere in the writings of the New Testament do we find a more moving exposition of this process than in the eighth chapter of Paul's letter to the Romans. Up to this point, not the work of the Spirit, but the redeeming death of Jesus has been the focus of Paul's argument concerning the way God establishes humans in right relationships with himself. But in Romans 5:5, he states, almost in passing, how Jesus' loving gift of service reaches us: 'hope does not disappoint us because God's love has been poured into our hearts through the Holy Spirit which has been given to us'. Please observe how confidently Paul makes this declaration. His confidence is rooted in the fact that he and his readers have actually been touched by this Spirit.

LIVING IN A NEW WAY

Now, in Romans 8, he develops the meaning of the statement that 'God's love has been poured into our hearts through the Holy Spirit'. The first thing that Paul emphasizes is the *power* of what he calls 'the newness of the Spirit' (7:6). In chapter 7, he sketched the dismal situation of humans apart from this power of God's love: even though they recognize the goodness of God's commandment, they are not able to be truly obedient because their freedom is enslaved by the power of sin: 'I serve the law of God with my mind, but with my flesh I serve the law of sin' (7:25). But now, says Paul, 'the Spirit of life in Christ Jesus' has set us free from the power of sin (8:2) so that those of us who 'walk in the Spirit' can keep the righteous requirement of God's commandments (8:4). Paul makes clear that the power of the Spirit is not an external or mechanical one, but influences our perception and our action: 'those who live according to the Spirit set their minds on the things of the Spirit' (8:5). Such a way of living, Paul insists, is possible 'if in fact the Spirit of God dwells in you' (8:9). Indeed, the work of the Holy Spirit in us now is an anticipation of our sharing in the resurrection of Jesus: 'If the Spirit of him who raised Jesus from the dead dwells in you, he who raised Jesus Christ from the dead will give life to your mortal bodies also through his Spirit which dwells in you' (8:11).

The connection between the gift of the Spirit and being formed in the image of Christ can hardly be stated more plainly: 'All who are led by the Spirit of God are sons of God. For you did not receive a spirit of slavery to fall back into fear, but have received the spirit of sonship. When we cry "Abba, Father", it is the Spirit himself bearing witness with our spirit that we are children of God' (8: 14–16). An astonishing proposition: the Holy Spirit who cries out in prayer from our hearts thus bears witness to our sharing in the life of Jesus, God's Son. Paul continues, 'and if children, then heirs of God and fellow heirs with Christ, *provided we suffer with him in order that we may also be glorified with him*' (8:17). I have emphasized these last two clauses to show how they encapsulate the transformative process that I have been proposing as the essential work of the Holy Spirit in human lives. The Spirit gives the power to live in a new way. That way is not the path of honour and glory and success, but the same path of service and suffering Jesus followed in his obedient response to God.

CONTACT

Paul thus sees Christian existence as one caught in the tension between the present power of the Spirit that enables us to endure the path of messianic suffering, and 'the glory that is to be revealed to us' that will mean 'the glorious liberty of the children of God' (8:18, 21). Creation groans in its agonies of new birth, Paul declares (8:22), 'and not only creation, but we ourselves, who have the first fruits of the Spirit groan inwardly as we wait for adoption as sons, the redemption of our bodies' (8:23). The suffering is real. The glory is not yet ours. Another passage from Paul should be inserted here: 'Though our outer nature is wasting away, our inner nature is being renewed every day. For this slight momentary affliction is preparing for us an eternal weight of glory beyond all comparison . . . he who has prepared us for this very thing is God, who has given us the Spirit as a guarantee' (2 Cor. 4: 16–17; 5:5).

And here is what is most remarkable: the Holy Spirit participates with us in this agonizing transformation of our human existence and of creation itself. Here is, truly, 'the love of God poured into our hearts', for a deeper intimacy between the divine and the human spirit can scarcely be imagined than one in which

God's spirit enters into the agony of human suffering. The Spirit is not passive in the process, but active: 'Likewise the Spirit helps us in our weakness; for we do not know how to pray as we ought, but the Spirit himself intercedes with us with sighs too deep for words. And he who searches the hearts of men knows what is the mind of the Spirit, because the Spirit intercedes for the saints according to the will of God' (8:26–27; compare 1 Cor. 2:11–12).

The Holy Spirit pervades the pages of the New Testament as the power of new life and personal presence and the transformation of human existence. In those pages, and in our lives, the Holy Spirit is the symbol for the touch of contact between the divine and the human spirit.

Chapter 14

John the Baptist: Prophet of the Great Reversal

Each of the canonical Gospels interprets the ministry of Jesus in the light of his death and resurrection. Each also shapes its image of Jesus by engaging some aspect of the symbolic world of Torah. In Luke-Acts (the two-volume composition now read as the Gospel of Luke and the Acts of the Apostles), it is the prophetic dimension of Torah that most obviously shapes Luke's characters and narrative. It is within this overall prophetic context that Luke portrays John the Baptist as the prophet of God's great reversal.

Prophetic imagery pervades Luke's entire composition, which was written to persuade Gentile believers that, despite the failure of many Jews to accept Jesus as their Messiah, God had proven true to his promise to Israel, by bringing about a 'restored people' in the form of the first Christian community in Jerusalem. Because of that fulfilment of God's prophetic word, Gentile readers also could 'have assurance in the things about which [they] had been instructed' (Luke 1:4). God both makes and keeps promises. The prophetic word invariably is accomplished.

LUKE'S PORTRAYAL OF CHARACTERS

In Luke-Acts, 'the things brought to fulfillment among us' (Luke 1:1) include not only the prophetic words in Scripture – including the law of Moses, the prophets, and the psalms (Luke 24:44) – but also the words spoken within his own narrative, for Luke portrays all his major characters as prophets. Most obviously, Jesus appears as a prophet like Moses (Acts 3:22–23; 7:37). Like Moses, he was sent a first time to save his people, but because they were ignorant, he was rejected (Acts 7:23–29). As Moses was empowered by God to go to his people a second time and lead them to freedom (Acts 7:33–39), so does Jesus, empowered by the Holy Spirit through his resurrection, 'visit the people' once more with a second offer of salvation, this time through the Spirit-filled prophetic words and deeds of his apostles.

In Luke's Gospel, Jesus is a prophetic Messiah, who is filled with the Holy Spirit (Luke 4:14–20), speaks God's word (Luke 8:11, 21; 11:27–28), does signs and wonders among the people (Luke 24:19; Acts 2:22) and creates a division between those open to God's message and those closed to it (Luke 2:34). So also his followers who receive the Holy Spirit at Pentecost (Acts 2:1–5) are filled with the spirit of prophecy (Acts 2:18), speak God's word with signs and wonders (Acts 4:29–30), and create a divided response among the people (Acts 4:1–4). Jesus and his followers, in turn, are part of a prophetic tradition that begins with Moses, extends through Elijah, Elisha and David, and finds its most recent and impressive realization in the prophetic forerunner to Jesus, John the Baptist.

JOHN THE BAPTIST

As a historian, Luke could scarcely avoid dealing with John, for he was a formidable historical figure in his own right. Josephus devotes a lengthy paragraph to John in the eighteenth book of his *Jewish Antiquities*, noting that it was his popularity with the people that led Herod to execute him. Luke himself tells us that John the Baptist had followers some 20 years after the death of Jesus as far away from the Jordan as Ephesus. They had been baptized with John's baptism, but had not heard of that associated with Jesus (Acts 18:25; 19:1–7). All of the evangelists, in fact, reveal a certain amount of what can be called the 'anxiety of influence,' by the way they portray John almost completely with reference to Jesus, downplaying any independent ministry he might have had.

Some of that same anxiety might account for some of the peculiarities of Luke's portrayal of John. For one thing, he can't seem to keep John in place once and for all. Luke mentions John more often then any other New Testament composition; his name not only appears 22 times in the Gospel (compare 16 in Mark, 23 in Matthew, and 18 in John), but also 9 more times in Acts! From the first mention of John to the last, furthermore, Luke always pairs him with Jesus. In the infancy account, the annunciation and celebration of John's birth are deliberately contrasted to that of Jesus (compare Luke 1:13–17, 68–80 with 1:26–56 and 2:1–51). John is great, but Jesus is greater. The same distancing effect might also be detected in the fact that, alone of the synoptic evangelists, Luke does not report the death of John (where John holds the scene alone), only alluding to it in passing (Luke 9:7–9). And in the baptism of Jesus, Luke so marginalizes John's participation that it almost appears that he was not present (see Luke 3:19–21)!

Yet, clearly Luke does not intend to diminish John's importance. As do Matthew and Mark, he has Jesus declare, 'I assure you, there is no man born of woman greater than John' (Luke 7:28). And the effect of his bringing John on the scene time after time is not to lessen but to increase John's presence. So is his minute attention to John's annunciation and birth; in Luke's version, John and Jesus are cousins! What, then, is Luke's odd portrayal of John up to? We can begin by observing two further remarks made by Jesus in the passage just quoted. The first states that John is 'a prophet and something more than that' (7:26); the second asserts, 'the least born into the kingdom of God is greater than him' (7:28).

THE BAPTIST'S DISTINGUISHED PROPHETIC ROLE

The special prophetic role played by John in Luke's story makes John a hinge figure. He is on one side a prophet like those of old who announce God's judgment on an unrepentant Israel and calls it to repentance. Yet, on the other side, 'the word of God' that came to John in the desert (3:2), and which he preached to all who came to him, is called by Luke, 'proclaiming the good news' (3:18). Notice the deep ambiguity in Jesus' declaration, 'The law and the prophets were in force until John. From his time on, the good news of God's kingdom has been proclaimed, and people of every sort are forcing their way in' (16:16). John is where the 'law and prophets' and the 'good news' meet; he is a prophet both of the old and the new covenant.

John, then, is literally a pivotal figure in Luke's narrative, a prophet in whose ministry ages both meet and are differentiated. John is filled with the Holy Spirit from the womb (1:15) and shows it by leaping in Elizabeth's womb at the recognition of Mary's carrying the Messiah (1:44). John is to 'bring back many sons of Israel' and 'prepare a people for the Lord' (1:16–17). He is to 'go before the Lord to prepare straight paths for him' (1:76). Yet, he is also to give that people 'knowledge of salvation through forgiveness of sins' (1:77). No wonder that Luke keeps returning in his narrative to John both as the point of ending and the point of beginning (see especially Acts 1:5, 22; 10:37; 11:16; 13:24, 25).

But John is a point of pivot in another way. Luke's greatest tribute to John is to provide him with a prophetic ministry of his own, and makes it *John's* announcement of God's word that the time of great reversal has now begun. In this light Luke's otherwise strange placement of John's arrest before the baptism of Jesus (Luke 3:20), leaving the impression that John may not even be present at Jesus' baptism in Luke 3:21, is seen to serve another purpose. John is given the dignity of having a full ministry like other prophetic figures; he is not reduced to being the forerunner of Jesus. Jesus' baptism, furthermore, now appears as a direct prophetic investiture by the Holy Spirit, rather than simply a human ritual (3:22).

We notice, then, it is at the point when John begins his prophetic ministry that Luke lists all the rulers from Caesar on down (3:1–2). With John, the story of Israel intersects the larger world history. John's prophecy, however, is not an attack on those worldly orders. Instead he proclaims 'a baptism of repentance for the forgiveness of sins' (3:3). Part of the tradition inherited by Luke (see Mark 1:4), John's message appears in his story as the fulfilment of the Zechariah's prophecy that he would 'give his people a knowledge of salvation in freedom from their sins' (Luke 1:77). The word of God, then, calls for a reversal. It is first of all, however, not a changing of the structures of society, but a changing in the attitudes of the heart.

HOW JOHN THE BAPTIST PREACHED 'A CHANGE OF HEART'

The call of God to repentance does, nevertheless, have social implications. Luke follows Mark in citing Isaiah 40: the herald's voice is preparing a path in the wilderness for the Lord (Luke 3:4; compare 1:76). But in contrast to both Mark and Matthew at this point, Luke continues the citation to include the imagery of the low being lifted up and the high brought low (Luke 3:5). This is the reversal. But what is its social effect? First, we see that Luke also includes from Isaiah the statement, 'and all flesh shall see the salvation of God' (3:6). Here we find an intimation of the Gentile mission: all humans will have access to God's salvation. This theme reaches its conclusion at the end of Acts, when Paul declares to Jewish leaders in Rome: 'This word of salvation has been sent to the Gentiles. They will believe it' (Acts 28:28). Repentance will be available to all (compare Luke 24:47); the people of God, in other words, will include more than Jews.

The Jewish people itself, furthermore, will be divided on the basis of this message. This is made clear by two of John's judgement sayings. He warns the Jewish crowds that had come to him not to rely on the claim that they were Abraham's children (that is, part of the Jewish people). The reason is: God can raise up children even from stones (Luke 3:8) – that is, anyone who repents in the heart can belong.

What is needed, then, are 'fruits of repentance' (3:8), that is, actions showing that one has a changed heart. Using an agricultural image John says that any tree that is not fruitful will be cut down and thrown into the fire (3:9). Those who do not respond to the prophetic message, in other words, will not be part of the restored people of God even if they are Jewish by heritage. A fundamental redefinition of membership in God's people is at work here; it is not a matter of birth or culture, but a matter of a religious and ethical response. In the judgement saying of 3:17 John promises that the one coming after him (the prophet Jesus) will divide the people even more decisively: 'His winnowing fan is in his hand to clear his threshing floor and gather the wheat into his barn; but the chaff he will burn in unquenchable fire.'

Just as the crowd will ask Peter after Pentecost (Acts 2:37), Luke has this crowd ask John, 'What should we do?' (Luke 3:10), and John responds with samples of ethical instruction – all of them, we note, dealing with the use of possessions (Luke 3:10–14) – that anticipate Jesus' later sermon on the plain: in short, don't take what is not yours, and share what you have with others. In response to the prophet John, as in response to the other prophets in his composition, the way people use possessions symbolizes their response to God's call to a changed life. Luke rightly calls this a 'preaching of good news' (3:18).

SUMMARY

By having John anticipate the message of Jesus, Luke makes the simple point that God's word poses the same challenge in every age: God calls not first of all for a change of government or a change in society, but for a reversal of human values in human hearts, a change of attitude that issues in real actions having to do with possessions and their use. Those who respond to this challenge with the 'fruits of repentance' are, no matter who they are or where they are from, a part of God's people, the children of Abraham. Those who fail to respond with a change of heart and action are, no matter what their place in society or Church, not a part of the people that God creates on earth as a laboratory of human possibility.

Chapter 15

How Saint Luke
Affirms the World

New Testament scholarship has only slowly caught up with the instinctive wisdom of the long-ago teachers who determined the shape of the canon by their answer to second-century challenges put to the community's traditional collection. In response to Marcion, who thought only Paul's version of Christianity correct and insisted that a gospel had to match Paul's supposed doctrinal purity, the great Church included four gospels of obviously diverse perspective, signifying that something other than doctrinal consistency made them valuable to Christian life. In response to Tatian, who found the multiplicity of the Gospels a scandal and constructed from the four traditional narratives the first gospel harmony which he called the *Diatesseron*, the great Church asserted that all four Gospels were to be retained despite their points of disagreement on historical detail. The canonizers perceived that the Gospels were important not as sources for the life of Jesus, but as witnesses and interpretations of Jesus for the Church.

To take the canon of the New Testament seriously means to read and appreciate the Gospels in all their plurality. Within their diversity of fact and perspective, each bears truthful witness. None of the Gospels uniquely contains the truth about Jesus or the meaning of discipleship; none is utterly wrong. They are to be valued as much for the ways in which they diverge as for the ways in which they agree.

When New Testament scholars engage in the literary analysis of a particular gospel, therefore, they respect the canonical shape of the text. If each gospel teaches the Church through its own irreducibly valuable voice, then we must pay attention not only to what each says but also to the ways in which it speaks. Religious message and literary shaping are inextricably joined, so that attending to the literary voice of a gospel is in effect preparing to be instructed by it. Within the Church, literary analysis of the New Testament is less in service to aesthetics than to faith.

THE LITERARY UNITY OF LUKE-ACTS

The literary analysis of Luke-Acts has been particularly slow in developing. The designation 'Luke-Acts' – for the Gospel according to Luke and the Acts of the Apostles – recognizes a literary unity that the canonizers and virtually the entire history of interpretation neglected. Luke was placed with the other synoptic Gospels and looked so much like them that it was interpreted in isolation from its sequel. Acts followed the Gospel of John and preceded the Letters of Paul, so was treated as a separate historical treatise. Luke was read for the life and teachings of Jesus, Acts for the history of the primitive Church. Although everyone acknowledged that Luke authored both volumes, few interpreters thought through the implications of that acknowledgment.

But in fact Luke-Acts is an intrinsic literary unity. If its distinctive voice is accurately to be heard, it must be followed through both volumes. The prologue introducing each volume and a multitude of literary interconnections joining the Gospel and Acts suggest that we not only have two books that happen to have been written by the same person, but also a single literary project. Luke used Mark as a source for his Gospel story, but then in Acts deliberately set out to continue the story of Jesus in the story of the Church.

Luke's success can be measured by the fact that generations of readers have considered things to have happened just the way he described them, and have failed to recognize that the sense of natural sequence and continuity between the ministry of Jesus and the mission of the early Church owes everything to the literary artistry and theological insight of Paul's excellent student, Luke.

APOLOGETIC

As the form of his prologues makes clear, the literary genre Luke employed for his purposes was that of historical narrative. Ancient historiography always had a moral purpose, and Luke's account of the messianic movement would be recognized in the first-century Mediterranean culture as an example of apologetic history, doing for nascent Christianity what the writings of Josephus and Philo had accomplished for diaspora Judaism. Apologetic literature had more than one purpose. The obvious goal was to make an alien tradition intelligible to the dominant culture. But by using the categories of outsiders to explain it, the very attempt also served to reinterpret the tradition. Luke's apologetic history is addressed even more directly to insiders than to outsiders. Luke's goal is not so much the defence of Christianity against the State as it is the defence of God's ways to believers whose recent experience could well have raised serious doubts about God's truthfulness and reliability.

Even the most casual reader recognizes that at one level Luke-Acts celebrates the extension of God's Word to the Gentiles. Luke's intended readers are in all likelihood Gentile Christians, and the narrative of how the Gospel moved 'from Jerusalem to Rome' (Acts 1:8) serves as an etiological myth for Gentile Christianity. Luke's readers are among those who, unexpectedly, have received the 'salvation of God' and have believed (Acts 28:28). But Luke's readers also know that the spread of the Gospel to the Gentile world was, if not the direct result, nevertheless involved with the rejection of the gospel by many of the Jews.

In stark terms, here is the problem: God had made his promises to Israel (Luke 1:68–74; Acts 3:25–27; 7:3–8). If the Jews have not now received the promised blessings – and appear ever less likely to receive them, since the Jewish mission appears over – God has failed to keep his word. The failure of God's fidelity to his promises is as much a problem for the Gentiles as for the Jews. Why should they have confidence in a God who is capable of reneging on his promises? If God after such a long and tumultuous relationship could so easily abandon the children of Abraham, why should the Gentiles trust his present affection for them?

Luke's apologetic history therefore seeks to provide his Gentile believers with 'assurance' (*asphaleia*) concerning the things in which they have been instructed (Luke 1:4) by showing through the narrative how God had 'brought to fulfillment' (Luke 1:1) all the things He had promised. Luke's literary and religious purposes are closely connected to the 'order' or 'sequence' of events in his narrative (Luke 1:3). His narrative shows that during his earthly ministry not all Jews rejected Jesus as the Messiah, but only the leaders. Indeed, many of the simple people and the outcasts gladly received Jesus (Luke 7:39–30; 15:1–2). He demonstrates further that the first church in Jerusalem was composed precisely of such a faithful community of Jews, for whom God fulfilled the promises to Abraham by pouring out upon them the Holy Spirit, creating a restored Israel headed by the twelve apostles (Acts 2–4). When the Good News travelled beyond Jerusalem to the Samaritans (Acts 8) and eventually to the Gentiles (Acts 11–15), therefore, it did so as a natural and harmonious continuation of the gift given to the faithful Jews. Luke's narrative shows that Gentile Christianity is an extension rather than a replacement of Israel as God's people, and that God's fidelity to the promises is revealed precisely in this sequence of events.

CONTROL OF MATERIAL

Such a summary does not do justice to the New Testament's most literarily self-conscious composition. Luke's narrative argument – spanning both volumes and joining them together – cannot without distortion be reduced to simple propositional terms. The actual reading of the narrative in sequence unfolds the richness of Luke's literary imagination and the depth of his religious perceptions. Not only in the thrust of his central argument but also in the detailed shaping of every detail we find an author in complete and confident control of his materials.

Notice how effectively, for example, Luke has made the use of prophetic imagery work as an organizing device. Jesus and his followers are portrayed as prophets: filled with the Holy Spirit, they speak God's Word with boldness and work signs and wonders, thereby bringing God's 'visitation' to the people (Luke 24:19–20; Acts 2:22; 6:8). But their words and deeds also create a division among the people. They experience both acceptance and rejection. However, since they are God's spokespersons, those who reject them also reject God's Word (Luke 10:16). Luke finds in Moses, the first and greatest of Israelite prophets (Deut. 18:15–18; 34:10–12), the model for his prophetic characterization. Jesus is therefore the 'Prophet like Moses' (Acts 3:22–23). God sent him to the people for their salvation, but ignorant of God's plan, they rejected him a first time just as Moses had been in the time of the Exodus (see Acts 7:17–29). But just as Moses was sent back a second time in power to save the people (Acts 7:30–37), so was Jesus. After his resurrection to God's power, Jesus continued to work through his prophetic successors, the apostles, by means of the Holy Spirit, offering salvation to those willing to accept it (Acts 3:13–16; 4:23–31). The prophetic parallel enables Luke to hold together the diverse parts of his story and create a narrative that has considerable dramatic tension: will the people offered a second chance to accept the prophet in fact do so?

Luke works his subsidiary themes into his basic argument with great effectiveness, resulting in a certain definite tone to his narrative. When one steps back from the details of the text to view it from a larger perspective, it is clear that Luke combines in remarkably creative tension two distinct yet interrelated messages. One is an optimistic affirmation of the world. The other is a vigorous challenge to the world. Luke's affirmation of the world can only be sketched in the broadest terms here, but it is one of the most characteristic and attractive features of his canonical witness.

LUKE'S AFFIRMATION OF THE WORLD

The simplest observation here may get us quickest to the essential point: Luke is the least apocalyptic of the New Testament writers. His eschewing of the apocalyptic mode is perhaps most evident in his editing of the 'Little Apocalypse' in Mark 13:1–36 (compare Luke 21:5–36), but it pervades his entire narrative. The very writing of a historical account, in fact, takes a stand against a radically apocalyptic view of reality. Luke does not view the world as still in the inexorable grip of satanic forces until a climactic turnaround marks the end of history. God has never been absent from the world. The God who made the promises to the patriarchs has been constantly at work to visit and save his people. God's fidelity is shown above all in the sending of the prophets. Jesus is the greatest but not the first prophet. He stands in the line of Moses and Elisha and Elijah. And the spirit of prophecy released by Jesus continues to work through the apostles and their successors. As God worked 'signs and wonders' for the people in the past through Moses, so he did also through Elijah and Elisha (Luke 4:25–27; 7:1–16). These same powerful deeds were worked also by Jesus, and again by the apostles. In such healings and exorcisms carried out in diverse times and places, the rule of Satan over human hearts is progressively subverted and the Kingdom of God established (Luke 4:1–12; 11:14–26; Acts 5:1–11; 8:20–24; 13:4–12).

Luke is also the least gnostic of New Testament writings. He does not view the physical world as a dangerous or profane place that needs to be abandoned in order to reach God, or physical processes as the deceptive stagecraft of an evil God, or the passage of time as the theft of authentic being. Once more, the act of writing an historical account itself represents a validation of the physical world with its bodies and its intrinsically temporal character. It is not by accident that Luke of all the canonical Gospels has the most intricate and human-centred birth accounts, for he is the evangelist most committed to the implications of the incarnation.

Salvation comes from a real human being born of real parents, who live not in a Never-Never Land of fantasy, but rather in the specific times and places and struggles locatable by historical inquiry (Luke 1:5; 2:1–6; 3:1–2). Luke's concern to get the events 'in sequence' is not simply a matter of rhetorical effectiveness; it reflects rather the conviction that the divine purpose is accomplished not apart from but through the very processes of human causality.

THE HUMAN BODY

Luke's positive assessment of the physical world created by God is shown by such simple things as the role played by food and drink. Jesus is no ascetic. In fact, the charge against him by his opponents is that he is a glutton and a drunkard and a friend of sinners (7:34)! In the Lukan parables, Jesus uses the banquet as an image of joy over human reconciliation (15:22–32), as well as an image of joy shared between God and humans (13:29; 14:15–24). In Luke's portrayal of Jesus' ministry, Jesus does indeed spend a great deal of time at banquets, both with his followers and opponents (5:29–39; 7:36–50; 14:1–11). It is at a meal, and through the sharing of bread and wine, that Jesus reveals to those followers the deepest meaning of his identity as 'the one among you who serves' (Luke 22:14–38), and it is at meals with his disheartened followers that he reveals himself to be alive in a new and even more powerful fashion (Luke 24:30–43; Acts 1:4; 10:41).

Luke has the same positive view of the human body in all of its glories and frailties. Luke notes the 'strips of cloth' with which Jesus is wrapped in the manger (Luke 2:7), and has John the Baptist's first prophecy be a kick within Elizabeth's womb (1:4)! Luke may not have been a physician, but he had a keen eye for all the symptoms of human illness brought before Jesus and the apostles (Luke 4:38; 6:18; 9:39; Acts 3:1–7; 5:15–16). In the healing touch of the prophets, Luke sought to portray the healing of a people (Luke 7:22; 13:16–17). And in the risings up and rejoicing and even dancings of those healed, he saw the symbol for the power of resurrection at work in the world (Luke 5:24–26; 7:16; Acts 3:8–10, 13–16). Luke is therefore far from embarrassed by the physical manifestations of the resurrected Jesus, or the physical miracles worked by the apostles.

In the same way Luke views the way humans use their physical possessions as a symbol for their self-disposition before God. People show their closedness to God's visitation by being 'rich' and clinging to their possessions (Luke 6:24; 14:15–24; 16:14, 19–31). In contrast, people show their openness to God by being 'poor' and willing to share their possessions (Luke 1:53; 4:18; 6:20; 14:26–33; 21:1–4). It does not surprise us therefore to see the first community in Jerusalem signal its spiritual unity by its complete sharing of possessions (Acts 2:41–47; 4:32–37).

Such perceptions of the physical world derive from a fundamental understanding of the world as created by God. For Luke this means that an essential aspect of God's fidelity is the way in which all humans can come to a knowledge of God through the created order. God's revelation is not restricted to the Jews or to the texts of Torah. God 'has not left himself without witness' among all peoples (Acts 10:34; 14:17). The Gentiles too can from the powers of nature and the movements of their own hearts 'seek God, perhaps even sense and find him. Indeed he is not far from each one of us, "for by him we live and move and are"' (Acts 17:27–28).

GENTILES AND JEWS

Luke's affirmation of the world is revealed also in his positive outlook on outsiders to the messianic movement, an openness absent from the apocalyptic and gnostic perspectives, each of which capitalizes on 'insider' status. Luke lacks entirely the xenophobia toward Gentiles that Matthew carried over from Judaism; indeed, much of Luke's story is meant to show how the Isaian prophecy that 'all flesh will see the salvation of God' (Luke 3:6; Isa. 40:5) has been worked out through the vagaries of historical events. In Luke's narrative, the Gentiles are portrayed much like the outcasts among the Jews whose poverty and marginalization made them hungry for the prophetic word: in fact, the deepest insight reached in the Church's process of deciding on the legitimacy of the Gentile mission (Acts 10–15) was that far from being second-class citizens, the Gentiles are full sharers in the gift of God with the Jews (Acts 15:11–21).

Neither, however, does Luke exalt the status of the Gentiles at the expense of the Jews. Luke is no anti-Semite and no Marcionite. The greatest portion of his narrative argument is taken up with showing how God had shown fidelity to his people by restoring Israel. Such a preoccupation is unintelligible unless Luke was deeply committed to the symbols of Torah within which alone the promises of God to this people are found. The majority of the Jews in Luke's narrative are receptive to the prophetic message (Luke 19:48; 21:38; 23:48). He portrays the leaders of the Jews as the ones who reject Jesus and the messianic movement (Acts 4–5).

Despite Paul's ritual threefold turning to the Gentiles in the latter portion of Acts (13:46; 18:6; 28:28), and the final application of the Isaiah 'blindness' passage against the Jewish leaders of Rome (28:25–27), Luke never suggests that the Jewish people as such are outsiders to God's plan. Nor, as his portrayal of Paul makes clear (Acts 21:20–21; 26:4–8), does he envisage a destruction of Jewish identity even within Christianity. The apostolic council does not demand circumcision of the Gentile converts (Acts 15:19), but neither does it forbid circumcision for Jewish converts (see Acts 16:3). For Luke, Gentiles and Jews alike have their own legitimate *ethos* ('customs') which do not advance them with God but do shape their cultural identities. Insofar as these are compatible with the good news, they can be maintained.

A SOCIAL REALITY

Consistent with such views, Luke has a positive attitude as well toward the structures of human society. The Roman Empire, for example, is not the Great Beast or the Whore of Babylon.

Luke recognizes that it has its deficiencies and corrupt administrators (Acts 24:26), but he shows no hostility to the fact of human governance. If anything, he regards the Empire as helpful to the Christian movement. In the same fashion, Luke appreciates the fact that Christianity, like the Judaism from within which it emerges, is not a religion of individual transformation, but a social reality, an 'assembly' (*ekklesia* = church) with structures and leadership and processes for making decisions and carrying out actions (Acts 14:23; 15:6–22; 20:17). Luke also shows the most remarkably subtle appreciation for the lubricants that made the machinery of society work. He knows the role of patronage and benefaction as well as the importance of friendship throughout the Graeco-Roman world (Luke 22:25; 23:6–12; Acts 19:31). He is not in the least embarrassed to describe the first Christian community in terms of a Greek philosophical school in a founding story like those found in Plato: the first believers are friends who held all their possessions in common (Acts 4:32–37)!

Perhaps the most obvious indication of Luke's positive appreciation of the world is in the care he has taken with his own literary composition. From the smallest vignettes to the architecture of the narrative as a whole, from his recasting of the stories and symbols of Torah to his appropriation of the literary motifs of Hellenism, from the smallest corrections of Mark's style to his passion for a story that communicated 'assurance' through its being told 'in order', Luke states in the most vivid fashion his conviction that human language and artistry are not unworthly instruments for God's revelation.

Is Luke-Acts, then, so much an affirmation of the world that it provides no challenge? By no means. In the next chapter I will try to show how Luke not only uses prophecy as a literary mechanism, but also speaks prophetically to the world.

Chapter 16

How Saint Luke Challenges the World

In the last chapter, I tried to show how the literary interpretation of Luke's overall narrative could reveal dimensions of his composition not otherwise obvious. By Luke's 'world-affirmation', I did not mean a Pollyanna-ish optimism about everything going on in the world, but rather a theological evaluation of creation – the physical order, time, society – implicit in the sort of historical account composed by the evangelist.

In writing a narrative about Jesus and Christian origins that connected the 'things fulfilled among us' (Luke 1:1) to the long history of Israel, and extended that story to the salvation of the Gentiles (Acts 28:28), Luke reveals himself to be an author with a profoundly non-apocalyptic outlook. The celebration within his narrative of the goodness of human bodies, of food and drink, of material possessions, of friendship within the social order, and of the access to God made possible both for Jews and Gentiles also shows us an author lacking entirely the world-denying and dualistic attitudes associated with gnosticism. Humans do not have to flee the world in order to seek God.

By no means, however, does Luke suggest that all is well in the world of human activity. He lacks the cosmic dualism of apocalyptic and gnostic imagination. But he retains the ethical dualism of the prophetic tradition. Although God creates the world good, human freedom frequently distorts creation. Thus the Gentiles who were given the opportunity to come to know God through the signs of nature actually ended up in 'the vain things' of idolatry (Acts 14:15). And the Jews who had been given Torah also turned its observance into a form of idolatry (Acts 7:42–50).

The idolatrous impulse is revealed in the patterns of behaviour that distort creation. Humans can become so preoccupied by their daily activities that they lose the sense of God's presence (Luke 12:16–21); can become so concerned to secure their lives by what they possess that they are incapable of responding to God's visitation (Luke 14:16–24; 17:30–33; 21:34), and end up losing what they had tried to secure. Humans can also turn religion itself into a closed system that serves mainly their own self-aggrandizement: piety something to be paraded (21:46–47), prayer a matter of peripheral vision (18:9–14), the keeping of God's commandments a claim to righteousness that requires no further 'comfort' from God (Luke 6:24; 18:18–24). Luke's observant eye notices all these ways in which humans resist the call of God implicit in the structure of creation.

THE PROPHETIC CHALLENGE

Luke's choice of prophecy as the central image of his work serves his double message well. Prophecy means more than the oracles spoken in the past that God now has brought to fulfillment. Prophecy is embodied in the figures of the prophets themselves. Moses, the first and greatest of Israelite prophets, is the exemplar (Acts 7:17–53). He is followed by Elijah and Elisha (Luke 4:25–27; 7:1–16; 9:30), then by John and Jesus, then by the Christian apostles and missionaries. They are all filled with the Holy Spirit, speak God's word with boldness, work signs and wonders among the people. The prophets, in short, are God's means of 'visiting his people' (Luke 1:68; 7:16; Acts 7:23; 15:14). The fact that God continues to send his prophets reveals his care for the world. The fact that his prophets experience rejection as well as acceptance shows that God's visitation, although intended for 'salvation' (Luke 1:68–79), also serves as a judgment.

The 'Word of God' that is spoken through the speech and

deeds of the Prophet Jesus poses a sharp challenge to the ways in which human idolatry has distorted the world. Luke shows us a Jesus who reaches out to the poor and the outcast as the essential expression of his mission (Luke 4:18–19), who heals all who seek to touch him (6:17–18; 8:43–48), who is willing to be friends with those who are morally and religiously suspect (Luke 5:8–10, 29–32; 7:34–50; 15:1–2). His gestures are the body language of God's universal care for creation, and emphatically state God's intention that 'all flesh will see God's salvation' (Luke 3:6).

In the same way, Jesus' words announce a reversal of human calculations and expectations. His announcement of 'blessings' on the poor, the hungry, the grieving and the oppressed (Luke 6:20–23) is accompanied by a corresponding set of 'woes' to those who now are rich, full, rejoicing and of good reputation (6:24–26). The parable of Lazarus and Dives spells out the reversal precisely: the rich man had his consolation in this life and spent the next in Hades. The poor man who was scorned in this life enjoyed the consolation of God's presence in the next (16:19–31). God's visitation through the Prophet does not confirm but rather confronts the conventional wisdom about human success.

RELIGIOUS PIETY

It also challenges the conventions of religious piety. At one level, Luke affirms the religious customs of the Jews. Jesus and his followers are portrayed as observant of the Law (Luke 2:22, 41–51; 4:16; 5:14; 22:7–11; 23:56). They interpret reality through the symbols of Torah (Luke 24:27, 44–46; Acts 2:17–21, 25–28; 13:33–41). The Temple is honoured as a place of prayer for the people (Luke 20:45–48; Acts 2:46; 3:1–6). But at another level, Luke criticizes any fidelity to religious custom, institution, or scripture that closes one to the visitation of God through the prophet. The pharisees and lawyers who are concerned to 'justify themselves' are not in fact regarded as righteous by God (18:9–14); in fact, they are an abomination before God (16:14–15). They show by their rejection of the prophets John and Jesus that they have

131

'rejected God's plan for them' (7:29–30). The members of the Sanhedrin who seek the death of Jesus and the apsotles and finally of Stephen in order to protect the honour of the temple and their customs are called 'stiff-necked people, uncircumcized in heart and ears [who] always resist the Holy Spirit' (Acts 7:51). Likewise, those Christians who insisted on Gentile converts being circumcized are regarded as 'testing God' (Acts 15:10).

Since for Luke God is the living God who creates the world at every moment (Acts 14:15; 17:24–26) and who knows the hearts of all people (Acts 1:24), the response to God's prophets rather than to scriptural precedents is the criterion of a genuine response to God. Those who refuse to accept the Prophet are themselves rejected from the people (Luke 10:16). Such is the case not only with the Jewish leaders who resisted Jesus (Luke 20:9–18), and the Diaspora Jews who rejected Paul (Acts 13:46–47), but also for the members of the messianic community who resist the prophetic authority of the apostles, as the monitory death of Ananias and Sapphira illustrates (Acts 5:1–11). At the same time, those who accept the prophets sent by God are also accepted by God into his people. The prophetic word that is judgment to the rich and powerful and self-satisfied is salvation to those who are poor and powerless and needy (7:50; 8:48). The divine reversal is expressed in the 'rise and fall of many in Israel' (2:34). As people respond to the prophet they demonstrate how 'the proud are brought low and the lowly are lifted up' (Luke 1:52; 14:11; 18:14).

THE CALL TO CONVERSION

The prophetic word does not only announce a state of affairs in which the poor are blessed and the rich are cursed. It demands a response from the hearer, a change in attitude and behaviour called conversion (*metanoia*). Jonah the prophet preached to the people of Nineveh and they converted (Luke 11:32). John the Baptist preached a baptism for conversion (Luke 3:3). So did Jesus himself (5:32), and his prophetic successors (Acts 2:38). They all demand of the hearers 'deeds (fruits) worthy of conversion' (Luke 3:8). What are they?

The Word of God spoken by the Prophet demands first of all a change of understanding. The distorted ways in which humans have measured values must be abandoned, and the measure by which God measures must be accepted as the measure of human life. Such is the point of Luke's Sermon on the Plain. If the Prophet announces a reversal of human expectations effected by God's visitation (Luke 6:20–26), so does he also demand that 'those who hear' adopt the values enunciated by that reversal.

They are no longer to act according to the standards of human wisdom, but by the measure of God's wisdom (6:43–49). In their relationship with God they can no longer seek to justify themselves, but in humility wait for the righteousness that comes from Him (Luke 18:9–14). In their relations with other humans, they can no longer practise the 'Go along to get along, you scratch my back, I'll scratch yours', morality of the idolatrous world. Rather, they must 'give to every one who begs from you; and of him who takes away your goods do not ask them again' (Luke 6:30); they are to 'be merciful even as your father is merciful' (6:36). What a daunting measure! But the Prophet assures his listeners that 'the measure you give will be the measure you get back' (6:38) – not from other humans, but from God!

THE DEEDS WORTHY OF CONVERSION

Luke's most inclusive term for the positive response to God's word is one shared with the broader Christian tradition. The fidelity that God has shown to the people in the fulfillment of his promises demands faith in return. For Luke, faith is not a matter only of a momentary or once-for-all decision. It is rather something that is to grow and mature. Characteristic in this respect is Luke's redaction of the parable of the sower (Luke 8:4–8) with its interpretation (Luke 8:9–15). The good seed that brings fruit to 'maturity' is a symbol for those whose faith is not temporary or superficial, but who 'hearing the word, hold it fast with the honest and good heart, and bring forth fruit with patience' (Luke 8:15). That term 'patience' is typical of Luke's perception. The world is not soon passing away, so fidelity to God entails perseverence through all the troubles of human existence (see 17:5–6). Luke's Jesus assures his listeners, 'by your patience you will gain your lives' (21:17).

Faith, in turn, means far more than belief, or even trust and obedience. It entails the imitation of the messianic Prophet, whose visitation is marked by sacrificial suffering. In Jesus' instruction concerning the necessity of his followers' suffering in the same way as the Son of Man, only Luke adds the word 'daily' to the imperative: 'If any one would come after me, let him deny himself and take up his cross daily and follow me' (Luke 9:22). Likewise, Luke has Jesus demand, 'whoever does not bear his own cross and come after me, cannot be my disciple' (Luke 14:27), and the verb tenses he uses make it clear that he means *'continue to bear* his own cross' (Luke 14:27). It is not by accident, then, that Luke shows the apostles and missionaries suffering rejection and persecution in the same way Jesus did (Acts 3–7). So Paul exhorted his new communities 'to continue in the faith, saying that through many tribulations we must enter the kingdom of God' (Acts 14:22).

EXEMPLARY LEADERSHIP

Luke is scarcely advocating a form of masochism. Suffering and rejection occur not because they are sought out as a validation of one's special status, but because the world has difficulties dealing with a faith which expresses itself in ways that threaten the stability of the world's own idolatrous systems. Think about the measure for leadership Luke holds out for the Church. Its missionaries are to travel without possessions, dependent on the generosity of others (Luke 10:4–8); or they are to work with their hands in order to support the needs of others (Acts 20:34–35). In either case, leaders of the community are to exemplify a leadership completely at odds with that common in the world: 'The kings of the Gentiles exercise lordship over them, and those in authority over them are called benefactors. But not so with you.

Rather let the greatest among you become as the youngest, and the leader as one who serves' (Luke 22:24–26). And this style of leadership is demonstrated most clearly in the mission of Jesus to the poor and the outcast: 'But I am among you as the one who serves' (Luke 22:27).

Think also how radical are the demands placed not only on leaders but on all those who belong to the restored people of God gathered by the prophetic word. In imitation of Jesus, they too are to extend their care beyond the comfortable limits of the familiar. They are to embrace those of foreign cultures and alien ideas (Acts 8–10) and are to accept them wholeheartedly into the community (Acts 11–15). They are to let go of the fear that makes humans cling to their possessions for security, and share their livelihood not only with each other, but with all who ask! Whereas the Greek proverb had it that 'Friends hold all their goods in common', and Luke felt comfortable describing the Christian community in just those terms (Acts 4:32–37), the demand of sharing extends beyond the support and spiritual unity of the community: Jesus tells his disciples, '*Make friends* with unrighteous mammon' (Luke 16:9). They are not to share only with those who can repay, but with all: 'give to everyone who begs from you' (Luke 6:30).

LET GO

How is such a radical openness and selflessness possible? Only by living within the measure of the prophetic word. Christians are not to live in fear about their daily needs (12:22) such as would lead them to build huge storage bins for all their possessions as a hedge against death. That is foolishness, for death comes to all (12:16–21). They are rather to live in a different sort of fear, of the God who 'after he has killed has power to cast into hell. Yes, I tell you, fear him' (12:5). If they live with reference to God, perceiving that it is from God that all they are and do derives (12:24–32), knowing that 'it is the father's pleasure to give you the kingdom' (12:32), they can then let go of the material possessions they had formerly used as a protection against anxiety: 'Sell your possessions and give alms. Provide yourselves with purses that do not grow old, with a treasure in heaven that does not fail . . . where your treasure is, there will your heart be also' (12:33–34). Likewise: 'Love your enemies and do good, and lend, expecting nothing in return, and your reward will be great, and you will be sons of the Most High; for he is kind to the ungrateful and the selfish' (6:35).

But to push the question still further, how can one persevere in such a demanding, perilous, self-sacrificing life of faith? The answer, for Luke, is to be found in a passage unique to his gospel. It is the parable of the widow and the unrighteous judge. He won't vindicate her but she wears him down by her importunateness, until he finally does her justice (Luke 18:2–7). That Luke understands this parable as a lesson for the life of *faith* is shown by his introduction and conclusion. He has Jesus conclude the parable: 'Will not God vindicate his elect, who cry to him day and night? Will he delay long over them? I tell you he will vindicate them speedily. Nevertheless, when the Son of Man comes, will he find faith on earth?' (Luke 18:7–8). And the parable, Luke tells the reader, is told 'to the effect that they ought always to pray and not lose heart' (18:1). In other words, for Luke, prayer is the very essence of the life of faith.

PRAYER

We are not surprised, therefore, to find prayer as one of the main sub-themes running through Luke-Acts. The Prophet Jesus is shown praying throughout his ministry, particularly at critical moments (see Luke 3:21, 5:16; 6:12; 9:28–29; 11:1; 22:32, 41–45; 23:46). Notice that Luke alone among the evangelists notes that Jesus was praying at his baptism (3:21) and at his transfiguration (9:28–35). He thereby suggests that these moments of uniquely intimate revelation concerning Jesus' identity as God's beloved Son came through the experience of prayer. It is also through prayer that he is able to fight through (the meaning of the term 'agony') his final testing before death (22:41–45), and in prayer that he entrusts his life to God at the terrifying moment of death (23:46).

Jesus also teaches his followers to pray (Luke 11:2–4; 18:1; 22:46), and in the gospel Luke provides splendid samples of prayer (Luke 1:46–56, 68–79; 2:29–32; 10:21–22; 22:42), showing how a people of faith is defined first of all by its relationship with God. Similarly in Acts, we are shown a community of prayer (see Acts 2:42–47; 3:1). The first community in Jerusalem is constantly in prayer as it awaits the gift of the Holy Spirit (Acts 1:14). It prays to make the proper decision concerning the replacement for Judas (1:24), and the seven who are to help the apostles (6:6). It is in prayer that Cornelius receives the vision telling him that he will be visited by Peter with a message of good news (10:2–4), and it is in prayer that Peter receives the vision that he eventually understands as the commission to preach to the Gentiles (10:9–16). Paul is in prayer after his frightening encounter with the risen Jesus, as he awaits the visitation of Ananias and instruction in the messianic faith (9:11). He is in prayer in the Temple when he becomes aware of his mission to the Gentiles (22:17). Above all, it is prayer that enables the apostles to endure persecution (4:23–31), Silas and Paul to survive imprisonment (16:25) and Paul to face his own trials and death with confidence (20:36). Prayer enables the life of faith because it is the fundamental 'conversion', a turning from the measure of the world and its power to the Word of God and its power.

We return then to the final way in which Luke's writing is an affirmation of the world, for it is by a faithful people's living by the measure of God's own compassion, and turning in prayer to the God who sustains all things, that the world finds its proper celebration as God's creation

Chapter 17

The Not-So-Empty Tomb (Luke 24:1–11)

Contemporary Christian readers know that the Gospel resurrection narratives are not simply to be equated with the experience and conviction that began the Christian religion and continues to enliven Christian identity. Resurrection faith concerns not a past event but a present power, not an occurrence in the empirical life of Jesus but the perduring presence of Jesus through the power of the Spirit in the community.

Christian readers therefore seek in each canonical account of the empty-tomb story a distinctive shaping of past traditions, which both bears witness to and interprets such ongoing experiences and convictions. Christian identity continues to be shaped by these texts, not by discovering the facts behind them, nor by tracing the stages of their transmission, nor by harmonizing them into an abstract message, but by struggling with the specific contours of each version. In the hard particularity of each account is the witness given.

The traditions of his followers' first encounters with Jesus' new and more powerful life are, furthermore, encountered by *us* only as embedded in consciously and artistically constructed narratives, which connect these traditions in multiple ways to the overall gospel story. The 'meaning' of the empty-tomb account in Luke 24:1–11 is not abstractable from its complex literary enmeshment. To assess Luke's account of the empty tomb means considering its role in his larger story.

In Luke's case, that role is literally pivotal. No other gospel gives the resurrection so central a narrative role as does the two-part narrative we call Luke-Acts. The entire argument concerning God's fidelity to the promises – what Luke calls 'the hope of Israel' (Acts 23:6; 24:15; 26:6–7; 28:20) – hinges on the resurrection of Jesus, the 'prophet whom God raised up' (Acts 3:23–26), as its pledge of fulfilment (Acts 17:31). Throughout the speeches of Acts, the apostles argue two intertwined points: the proper way to read Scripture is as prophecy (2:30–31; 8:34–35; 13:34; 24:14–15; 26:22, 27; 28:23); and when so read, Scripture points toward the resurrection of the Messiah as the means by which the blessings of Abraham are bestowed on the people (2:31–36; 3:25–26; 13:32–38; 23:6; 26:6–8, 23). Small wonder, then, that the resurrection event itself also receives extravagant attention in Luke's narrative. After this empty-tomb account (24:1–11), his gospel contains an unusually rich collection of appearance stories (24:12–49). Even after Jesus' ascension, Acts reports further appearances of the risen one to his followers (7:55–56; 9:3–9; 23:11; 22:17–21).

Luke's resurrection accounts reveal certain consistent preoccupations. One is the dialectic of absence and presence at the heart of resurrection faith. More than any other evangelist, Luke emphasizes the physical reality of the resurrected one: Jesus is not a ghost; he has flesh and bones (Luke 24:39); he can even eat and drink with the disciples (24:30, 42–43; Acts 1:6; 10:41). Yet at the same time, that physical presence can be misapprehended, or unrecognized (24:16, 35, 37); Jesus indeed can approach and withdraw with disconcerting unpredictability (24:15, 31, 36, 51). This theme is expressed most graphically in the uniquely Lukan tradition of Jesus' ascension (24:50–53; Acts 1:9–11). Jesus departs physically from the presence of his disciples, yet remains present to them in even more powerful new modes: through the gift of the Holy Spirit (2:33), in the works the Spirit enables 'through his name' (3:13–16; 4:29–31), in transformative and guiding visions (7:55–56; 9:3–9, 10–16; 22:17–21). Jesus is the same, yet different; Jesus has left, yet is more present than ever.

Equally dialectical is the interaction of divine agency and human interpretation. Luke makes heavy use of the machinery

of divine intervention: the two men at the tomb (24:4), later called
'angels' (or 'messengers' [*angeloi*, 24:23]), the two men at the
ascension (Acts 1:10), the portentous prophecies of the Risen
One (24:46–49; Acts 1:7–8). But at the same time, Luke shows
an impressive display of purely human emotional responses to
the events: the women at the tomb are puzzled (24:4); men are
'amazed' (24:12, 22) or 'disbelieve because of their joy' (24:41).
The disciples are shown to be in need of correction (24:5, 25–27,
39; Acts 1:7–8). Yet their incredulity (24:11), discussions (24:14),
recitations (24:19–24) and doubts (24:41) are all part of the process by which the human experience of Jesus' resurrection is
shaped. Luke particularly emphasizes the role of memory that,
jogged by these new encounters, discovers the true significance
of the prophetic words of Jesus (24:6, 44) and of the scriptures
(24:27, 44).

The previous two themes are comprehended by a third:
Luke's pattern of dispersal and gathering together. We are first
shown a series of disparate experiences: the women at the tomb
(24:1–11); Peter at the tomb (24:12); the disciples on the road to
Emmaus (24:13–32). But the experiences are joined by short
narrative exchanges: the women report to the eleven (24:11); the
disciples report the women's message (24:22), and they are told
of Peter's vision (24:34). Then Luke shows us all of the disciples
gathered in one place for the final appearance (24:36). As the
stories are traded and handed on, they gain both depth and
breadth from the contributions of other witnesses so that a
shared narrative of resurrection faith begins to take form. As a
common narrative emerges, the community itself simultaneously
takes form.

Luke had already begun to establish these themes in his
adaptation of the empty-tomb account that he found in his main
gospel source. He obviously considered Mark 16:1–6 inadequate
for his own purposes, for he added to it all these other traditions.
Nevertheless, he did keep it. Moreover, because the empty-tomb
account no longer held the same significance as it had in Mark's
account, where it served as the conclusion of an entire gospel,

Luke could exercise unusually bold editorial freedom. No part of Mark's version goes untouched. Because we possess both versions, Luke's alterations are clearly visible and provide secure access to the interpretation he gave to this strange tale.

The alterations that give Luke's version its distinctive character begin with the identity and role of the messengers. In Mark, the messenger is a 'young man', clearly meant to suggest the restoration of the disciples who had abandoned Jesus. The non-angelic, fully human identity of the messenger makes him the first witness of the resurrection and alleviates the failure of the women to fulfill their commission. In contrast, Matthew thoroughly supernaturalizes the event by making the messenger 'an angel of the Lord come down from heaven' who effects the rolling back of the stone, apparently in full view not only of the guards but of the women who had come to the tomb (Matt. 28:2–5).

Luke has neither young man nor angel but 'two men'. They are *not* identified here as angels (though that is the later report about them, 24:23). They are not the agents of the stone's being moved. Indeed, they 'come up on' the women who are puzzled by the discovery that the 'body of the Lord Jesus' is not there. In precisely the way such visitors function throughout Luke-Acts (Luke 1:11–13, 26–37; Acts 8:26; 9:10–16; 10:19; 16:9–10), these authoritative spokespersons help interpret the event. But who are they? Luke's diction in describing their 'shining clothes' recalls to the careful reader the 'two men' (Moses and Elijah) who conversed with Jesus at the transfiguration (Luke 9:30–31) as well as the 'two men' who interpret Jesus' ascension for the disciples (Acts 1:10). We recognize in these intertextual signals an allusion to Luke's presentation of Jesus as 'the prophet like Moses' whom God raised up. We remember, after all, that the topic of discussion between Jesus and the two men on the mount of transfiguration (supplied only by Luke) was the 'exodus' that Jesus was to accomplish in Jerusalem (9:31). The implicit message communicated by the reappearance of these two messengers is that this 'departure' is now being accomplished by Jesus' death, resurrection and ascension.

That Luke intended such an allusion is confirmed by the message delivered to the women. Here we find Luke's most dramatic alteration of Mark and the clearest expression of his own interpretation of the event. In contrast to Mark (and Matthew), the message does not seek to relieve their fear and says nothing about a future appearance in Galilee. Instead, the question 'Why are you seeking the one who lives among the dead?' (Luke 24:5) serves as something of a rebuke. In form as well as substance it reminds the reader of two other such questions in Luke's narrative: that of Jesus to his parents, 'Why is it that you have been seeking me?' (2:49); and (once more) that of these men to the disciples at the ascension, 'Men of Galilee, why do you stand looking into heaven?' (Acts 1:11). In each case, the question is accompanied by a clarification: Jesus declares that he must be about his father's affairs (Luke 2:49); the men state that Jesus will return again in the same way he was leaving (Acts 1:11). In this case, the men state: 'He is not here, but he has been raised.' The implicit suggestion is that they have failed to grasp the meaning of the event.

Rather than being commanded to deliver a message about a future appearance, the women themselves are invited to remember the past: 'How he spoke to you while he was still in Galilee.' The messengers quote to them (with only slight differences) Jesus' own passion prophecy from 9:22, a prophecy that concluded 'and on the third day rise'. Luke's 'correction' of Mark does more than eliminate a Galilean appearance and maintain Luke's geographical emphasis on Jerusalem as the place of Jesus' resurrection manifestations. It shifts the entire significance of the empty-tomb account. The 'absence' of Jesus is the premise for his 'presence' in a new form, for his absence is only 'among the dead' and his presence is to be among the living. This new thing, however, is not entirely new, nor should it have caused puzzlement. It had been prophesied by Jesus himself. In the most remarkable fashion, *the words of Jesus himself* provide the interpretive key to his absence among the dead.

With messengers and message, Luke makes the empty-tomb account a hermeneutical reflection: disappointed expectation leads to puzzlement, which provides an opening to discovery. But the way to discovery is through the maze of memory. What should have been heard the last time is now, in the shock of newness, heard, really heard, for the first time. Before there can be new sightings, there must be the cleansing of vision. The women are invited to perceive the Jesus of their past in a new way so that they can perceive him in a new way in their present as well.

This brings us to Luke's portrayal of the women. Consistent with his entire narrative, Luke presents the women in positive terms. They are persons of true piety: they observed the Sabbath rest 'according to the commandment' before coming to the tomb (23:56). They are also genuine disciples. They are the ones who had followed Jesus from Galilee and first exemplified the ideal of a community of possessions (8:1–3). In contrast to Peter, they had followed him faithfully to the scene of his death (23:49) and had borne witness to the place of his burial (23:55). They are uniquely capable of 'remembering' the entire sequence of events and thus of becoming the first human witnesses of the resurrection.

The women's behaviour is consonant with their role. When they discover that the body of the Lord Jesus is not in the tomb, they are not terrified but 'puzzled' (24:3; cf. 9:7; Acts 2:12; 5:24; 10:17), for the event itself is ambiguous, requiring interpretation. When confronted by the visitors, their fear and obeisance express an openness to the interpretation they are to receive (24:5). When they are told to 'remember', they *do* 'remember his words' (24:8). Moreover, even though they are not commanded to deliver this message to anyone else, these women, far from fleeing in mute silence (cf. Mark 16:8), proceed to tell 'all these things' to the remnant of the apostolic leadership (24:9).

It is only at this point that Luke provides the names of the women, because it is not in their mute witness of the empty tomb but in their having become 'ministers of the word' (Luke 1:2) that their real significance lies. Luke's positive portrayal of the women as trustworthy witnesses is all the more striking because it is placed in immediate contrast to the male rejection of the message. When the apostles hear the message from the women, they dismiss it. It appeared 'in their view to be so much nonsense'. Even Peter is only a partial exception, for when he runs to the tomb (24:12), he sees nothing and remembers nothing, returning only with 'amazement'.

The reader, however, should not be amazed. From the beginning, Luke has portrayed women as particularly good at accepting divine gifts that were humanly impossible (Luke 1:25, 38), as open to the surprising ways God subverted expectations, and as capable of 'turning things over in their hearts' in creative memory (2:19, 51). At the end of his gospel, as at the beginning, women demonstrate God's way of reversing human expectations, of 'lifting up the lowly' (1:52), and 'proclaiming good news to the poor' (4:18; 6:20). So when Luke begins his second volume, he is careful to include among those from Galilee praying in the upper room 'the women' (Acts 1:14), who will become with the gift of the Holy Spirit 'the daughters who will prophesy' (Acts 1:17) and proclaim 'the mighty deeds of God' (Acts 2:11). Here also, perhaps, for readers of today is a call to remembrance.

Part Three:

Jesus, The Heart of the Gospel

Chapter 18

The Search for (the Wrong) Jesus

The first half of this decade has been a busy one for questers after the historical Jesus. The Jesus Seminar capped a decade of self-promotion with the publication of *The Five Gospels: The Search for the Authentic Words of Jesus.*[1] Highly publicized forays into the search for Jesus were undertaken by amateurs like Bishop John Spong,[2] A.N. Wilson[3] and Stephen Mitchell,[4] as well as by such professional biblical scholars as Marcus Borg,[5] Barbara Thiering,[6] Burton Mack[7] and John Dominic Crossan.[8] In addition to the press coverage of the Jesus Seminar's regional camp-meetings and articles in major newspapers reviewing and assessing this 'New Quest,' the effort has been sufficiently noisy to attract attention in such unlikely quarters as the *Atlantic Monthly,*[9] the *Humanist,*[10] *GQ*[11] and *Lingua Franca.*[12] And far removed from the promotion mills, John Meier of Catholic University in Washington, D.C., has continued to toil away at the most monumental historical Jesus project of all.[13]

It is safe to say, I think, that all this commotion has created a general impression that the quest is important – although not because, as the Jesus Seminar publicity would have it, scholars will lose their jobs under pressure from reactionary Christians, and certainly not because these questers have come to such firm and unassailable conclusions that the guild of New Testament scholars should close up shop because nothing remains to be done. The opposite is the case – their portraits are wildly varied. In the crisp summary of T.W. Manson, 'By their lives of Jesus ye shall know *them*.'[14] Jesus appears in their pages as Qumran's wicked priest (Barbara Thiering), as a guru of oceanic peace (Stephen Mitchell), as a charismatic (Marcus Borg) and as a peasant Cynic (John Dominic Crossan).

The real significance of these highly public exhibits is that they have shown the wider world just how shaky some of the premises, and how shoddy some of the procedures, are in a great deal of biblical scholarship, both past and present. When I speak of shoddy practices, I have in mind more than the media manipulation of the Jesus Seminar, or the seminar's periodic pronouncements about who Jesus 'really was' before even a portion of the traditions dealing with him have been dealt with (until now the seminar has considered only Jesus' sayings, not his acts), or its failure in *The Five Gospels* even to apply its own criteria of authenticity consistently. I refer instead to the lack of true critical scholarship running – in varying degrees, to be sure – through all these publications.

With so many images of Jesus being produced, one would expect some embarrassment over a supposedly scientific method that yields such wildly divergent results, or some debate over what constitutes a legitimately derived image, or a demonstration of why one image should be preferred to another. In fact, practically nothing along these lines occurs. There is much assertion, little argument. Marcus Borg cites a poll he took among like-minded colleagues as his most substantial reason for seeking a 'noneschatological' Jesus.[15]

Working through this literature, I have not been able to make up my mind whether its colloquial and casual discourse is a function of sloppiness or of cynicism. I find what appears to be a deliberate sliding back and forth between two understandings of history. On the one hand, the authors claim to be doing 'critical scholarship,' without presupposition or bias, with the neutral assessment of sources, with the goal of simply discovering who Jesus 'really was'. On the other hand, they assume that this 'historical Jesus' should somehow be normative and that, in the light of their 'scholarly' deductions, Christianity needs to check its creed as well as its canon. Once more, the Jesus Seminar is an egregious example, claiming out of one side of its mouth that it is practising the most sober and critical research, yet from the other side of its mouth (both sides represented mostly by Robert Funk, chief spokesperson) claiming at the very outset of the project that it intends to use the assured results of scholarship to save Christianity from its evangelical captors.[16]

Apart from the usual and noteworthy exception of John Meier, one cannot find in any of these productions a critical reflection on the meaning of *history* itself, no consideration of its goals, methods or, above all, its limitations.[17] Such conceptual carelessness enables these books to offer the 'real Jesus' without ever engaging the truly difficult questions of the methods of historical knowing. Nowhere do these practitioners pause to consider that 'history' is not to be equated with 'reality', or that in fact 'history,' while important, is also a limited mode of human cognition, with a great deal of what all humans consider both 'real' and 'important' slipping through its rough sieve. To a remarkable extent, one finds in these tracts the same positivistic understanding of history that characterizes the fundamentalism they oppose. The authors fail to inform their readers that to state that the resurrection is not 'historical' – that is, it may not be demonstrable from historical sources – is not the same thing as to state that it is not 'real'. I am not altogether certain that the distinction has occurred to the authors themselves.

Beyond such shoddy practices, however, there is also the matter of shaky premises. Here we find that these Jesus books bring to the surface some dubious assumptions that have for too long been allowed to pass uncriticized within the scholars' guild. Perhaps a reason some scholars have been loath to criticize these productions – rather than simply hoping they might go away – is that they employ methods and moves widely used in the field but take them one step further, into obvious absurdity. It is time for the guild not only to reject the *reductio*, but also to recognize the *absurdum*, to which it has allowed free play for too long.

The popular publications claim to represent serious scholarship. Serious scholarship can rightly object to being tarred by the brush of self-promotion, meretriciousness, sloppiness and cynicism. The tone of the introduction to *The Five Gospels*, for example, combines messianism and hucksterism in equal measure, with the delusions of grandeur emitting a definitely paranoid aura. But is the scholarly guild prepared to face up to the fact that these Jesus books also reveal ways of doing business that are at best shaky and at worst plain silly?

Three such practices surface in virtually all these books, leaving one to wonder whether anything like recognizable historical research is going on.

The first is the way the hermeneutics of suspicion is applied to virtually everything in the New Testament and to virtually nothing outside it. The canonical gospels, one is led to think, are the least likely source of knowledge about Jesus. If they are to be used, they must be purified of later accretions or distortions brought from a faith perspective. They must be read in the light of apocryphal writings, or some earlier source excavated from within them, or some social-scientific model. Indeed, the only sources that *cannot* be referred to are the other writings of the New Testament!

Thus, despite the fact that Paul's letters are the earliest datable sources for anything about Christianity (c. 50–64 AD), and despite the fact that Paul's letters attest to a number of separate points in the Jesus story as found in the canonical gospels, and despite the even more striking point that Paul's *interpretation* of the Jesus story as one of radical obedience to God and self-donation to humans is precisely the same as that found in all four canonical gospels and only in them among all Jesus traditions, the evidence from Paul is not considered historically relevant.

What's going on here? Why shouldn't the earliest narrative sources and the even earlier testimony of Paul receive credit as historical evidence? The reasons are more ideological than historiographical. One is a commitment to a conflict model of earliest Christianity that goes back to the Tübingen School (mid-nineteenth century) but was given powerful new life over 30 years ago under the influence of Walter Bauer.[18] This model has elevated the legitimate perception of a diverse early Christianity into the dogma that it was a disparate movement of deeply opposed forces. In recent scholarship, furthermore, it seems as though none of these diverse Christian movements knew anything about any of the others. So Burton Mack (*The Lost Gospel*) can posit the 40-year development of a 'Q community' in Galilee completely untainted by any influence from either the Jerusalem church or the Pauline churches.

This flies in the face of the evidence of both Acts and Paul's letters, which, while candid about the tensions in the early movement, nevertheless show a remarkable level of communication and cooperation between leaders, including Paul. To avoid this problem, the current model must throw out most of Acts and expurgate much of Paul. But without the controls provided by these ignored sources, reconstructions quickly (as in the case of Mack) fly off into fantasy.

Paul in particular must be excluded from this recent Jesus research for another reason: in contrast to the Protestant theology that for years dominated biblical scholarship, in which Paul was the good guy who championed the principle of righteousness by faith, various liberation ideologies now dominate research. In these, Paul appears as the first and greatest enemy. In contrast to the itinerant Cynic peasant Jesus (imagined by John Dominic Crossan), Paul is the urban householder. In contrast to the woman-defined Jesus and the wisdom-driven Jesus movement (imagined by Elisabeth Schüssler Fiorenza), Paul is the proto-patriarch. In contrast to the gay magician Jesus (imagined by Morton Smith[19]), Paul is the hateful homophobe. In other words, to have an ideologically correct Jesus, we must exclude the complexity of an ideologically deviant Paul. But this, I need scarcely point out, is not critical history. It is the uncritical canonization of an ideological assumption.

A second tendency found not only in these Jesus books, but in New Testament scholarship as a whole, is, once these relatively stable controls have been excluded, an amazing confidence concerning the way pieces can be rearranged. The new questers claim to be able to determine, by means of various 'criteria', whether sayings attributed to Jesus are 'authentic'. They also claim the ability not only to detect within extant, unified, literary compositions a variety of earlier sources, but also to discern to the minutest detail various levels of redaction within such sources. Next they assume that behind every composition is a community and that one can move from the literary configuration of a text to the historical, social and ideological configuration of a specific community.

Armed with such assumptions, the Jesus Seminar can assert with unjustified confidence that Jesus could not have spoken certain parables or have made certain declarations. But for a long time, on the basis of just such circular and subjective criteria, determinations have also been made concerning which letters were 'really' from Paul or which undesirable parts of his letters must have been interpolations. In a similar fashion, the Jesus researchers can trumpet the isolation of the so-called Q Gospel (the material shared by Matthew and Luke but not found in Mark) as a discrete written source that can be subdivided into levels of redaction. But so have scholars for decades diced up the Pauline letters 2 Corinthians and Philippians into separate sources to be shuffled into different stages. Burton Mack can use the levels of redaction in Q to describe the history of a putative Jesus community in Galilee. Why not? The dissected pieces of Philippians were used by Willi Marxsen to 'reconstruct' the history of conflict in Philippi.[20] Similarly, the severed sources of 2 Corinthians have been used to 'trace the history' of Paul's relations with that church,[21] and the various stages of redaction in the Johannine corpus have been used to discourse confidently on the history of the Johannine community.[22] So the new questers follow this well-trodden path. None of this, however, is real history, but rather an elaborate paper chase. It is the result of an obsessive need to do history with sources inadequate to supply what is sought from them, leading to a distortion of historical method, chimerical historical reconstructions and the destruction of the only genuine witnesses for earliest Christianity we have, the discrete literary compositions of the New Testament.

The final tendency of the recent Jesus research – especially visible in Borg and Crossan – is the embrace of so-called social-scientific models. To paint his portrait of Jesus, Marcus Borg appeals to the sociological type of the charismatic *chasid*, which Geza Vermes posited on the basis of Honi the Circle Maker and Chanina ben Dosa from rabbinic literature.[23] John Dominic Crossan, on the other hand, appeals to the category of the peasant.[24] Having tossed out the narrative controls found only in the Gospels and the writings of Paul, models like these are obviously needed; no matter how many 'pieces' of the Jesus tradition are determined to be 'authentic', they cannot by themselves ever yield a profile of Jesus. No pile of pieces can ever reach meaning, for meaning can come only from pattern.

The same tendency we have observed in this Jesus research has also become prevalent in the study of earliest Christianity, where again there are too few pieces even to make a decent pattern, especially after the only narrative framework available, that of Acts, is thrown out as tendentious. To meet this void, some sort of 'scientific' model – anthropological or sociological – has been invoked to provide a pattern into which the pieces can be fitted. The need to do history demands that the pieces fit into some universally intelligible law of conflict or development. The result is that the unique is collapsed into the universal, the particular disappears into the general. Nothing new and surprising is encountered – only an instance of a universal law.

In the case of Jesus, the tendency allows this most distinctive and individual of humans only the range of possibilities available to a sociological abstraction. Jesus must think like a peasant, speak like a peasant, do what a peasant would do. Forget messianic consciousness or sense of unique sonship. He can't even be literate! The employment of such models enables the pieces to be put into a new combination, in place of the pattern provided by Paul and the Gospels. Is it a more 'historical' pattern? Only if one thinks that 'brandy-imbibing, cigar-smoking, British imperialist' adequately captures the significance of Winston Churchill.

Something other than disinterested historical research motivates these recent Jesus books. Present in all of them is a clear reformist goal, based on the conviction that traditional Christian belief is a distortion of the 'real' Jesus. Already with Paul, they hold, the Jesus movement was corrupted into the Christian religion. For Crossan and Mack, the distortion of Jesus' goals precedes the creed and is found in the narrative form of the canonical Gospels themselves. These scholars want a new understanding of Jesus and Christian origins to have an impact on the cultural phenomenon called Christianity by removing what Mack calls 'the privilege of the Christian myth'.[25]

This implicit – and sometimes explicit – theological agenda operates on two assumptions that have been around since the birth of the historical-critical method. The first is that historical knowledge is normative for faith: if historical research comes up with a 'different Jesus', then Christianity will have to change its ways.[26] The second is the assumption that a religion's *origins* define its religious *essence*, so that the first understanding of Jesus was better than any development of that understanding. But these are not properly historical observations. They are, rather, ideological commitments.

The production of such poor historiography and such confused theology in the same package suggests that these authors (like so many others in the biblical guild) are caught within some deep and unresolved conflicts concerning the proper or legitimate functions of critical biblical scholarship, and concerning the usefulness of an overarching historical model as the dominant paradigm for biblical studies.[27] After all, how much history can we really do with these ancient fragments? In their hands, what is called 'history' is really a camouflaged form of cultural critique of contemporary religious observance.

The frenzied dismantling of the narratives of the New Testament, the scavenging of 'usable pieces' from the wreckage, the pasting of such pieces into a new pattern derived from anthropology or some other social science – this effort increasingly appears to be an attempt to avoid or replace the unmistakable image of Jesus limned in the pages of the New Testament. The writings of Paul (and 1 Peter and Hebrews) and the canonical gospels converge in presenting an image of Jesus that is instantly graspable and has been unfailingly grasped by those whose lives have been transformed in its pattern.

This image, constructed by the narratives of the New Testament (including the narrative fragments of non-gospel compositions) and found *only* in these compositions as such (not in their pieces), is emphatically *not* the developed, dogmatic Christ of Church doctrine (true God and true man), nor is it the historical Jesus reconstructed from bits and pieces (true Cynic and true peasant). It is, rather, the etching of a certain human character, a model of the disposition of human freedom in obedience to God and in service to others, an identity so distinctive that it is readily grasped even in literary mimesis, like that of Dostoevksy's Prince Myshkin (in *The Idiot*) or Melville's Billy Budd.[28]

If critics within Christianity, or critics of Christianity, would openly challenge that image, not on the basis of its historicity but on the basis of its religious or moral coherence and adequacy,[29] something far more critical and interesting would be done with the New Testament than we find in the tired rationalist reductions that try to make history do criticism's work.

NOTES

1 Robert W. Funk, Roy W. Hoover and the Jesus Seminar (eds), *The Five Gospels: The Search for the Authentic Words of Jesus* (New York: Polebridge Press, 1993).

2 John Spong, *Born of a Woman: A Bishop Rethinks the Birth of Jesus* (San Francisco: HarperSanFrancisco, 1992) and *Resurrection: Myth or Reality?* (San Francisco: HarperSanFrancisco, 1994).

3 A.N. Wilson, *Jesus* (New York: Norton, 1992).

4 Stephen Mitchell, *The Gospel According to Jesus* (New York: Harper-Collins, 1991).

5 Marcus Borg, *Jesus, A New Vision: Spirit, Culture, and the Life of Disciple-ship* (San Francisco: Harper & Row, 1987); *Meeting Jesus Again for the First Time: The Historical Jesus and the Heart of Contemporary Faith* (San Francisco: HarperCollins, 1994) and *Jesus in Contemporary Scholarship* (Valley Forge, PA: Trinity Press International, 1994).

6 Barbara Thiering, *Jesus and the Riddle of the Dead Sea Scrolls: Unlocking the Secrets of His Life Story* (San Francisco: HarperSanFrancisco, 1992)

7 Although Mack's work is not explicitly part of this quest, his two major works are closely aligned to the methods and presuppositions surveyed here; see Burton Mack, *A Myth of Innocence: Mark and Christian Origins* (Philadelphia, Fortress Press, 1988) and especially *The Lost Gospel: The Book of Q and Christian Origins* (San Francisco: HarperSanFrancisco, 1993).

8 Most notably, John Crossan, *The Historical Jesus: The Life of a Mediterranean Jewish Peasant* (San Francisco: HarperSanFrancisco, 1991), *Jesus: A Revolutionary Biography* (San Francisco: HarperSan-Francisco, 1994); and *Who Killed Jesus? Exposing the Roots of AntiSemitism in the Gospel Story of the Death of Jesus* (San Francisco: HarperSanFrancisco, 1995).

9 Cullen Murphy, 'Who Do Men Say That I Am', *The Atlantic Monthly* (December 1986), pp. 37–58.

10 Kerry Temple, 'Who Do Men Say That I Am?', *The Humanist* (May/June 1991), pp. 7–15.

11 Russell Shorto, 'Cross Fire', *GQ* (June 1994), pp. 117–23.

12 Charlotte Allen, 'Away with the Manger', *Lingua Franca* (February 1995), pp. 1, 22–30.

13 John Meier, *A Marginal Jew: Rethinking the Historical Jesus*, 2 vols, (Garden City, NY: Doubleday, 1991–1994). Meier's work does not, in the main, fall under the summarizing comments I make in this article. For an appreciation and critique of his volumes, see my reviews, 'A Marginal Mediterranean Jewish Peasant', *Commonweal* 119 (April 1992), pp. 24–6; and 'Testing the Gospel Story,' *Commonweal* 121 (November 1994), pp. 33–5.

14 T.W. Manson, 'The Failure of Liberalism to Interpret the Bible as the Word of God', in *The Interpretation of the Bible*, ed. Clifford W. Dugmore (London: SPCK, 1944), p. 92.

15 Borg, *New Vision*, p. 20, n. 25; *Jesus in Contemporary Scholarship*, pp. 59–61.

16 See Funk's opening remarks in *Forum* 1/1 (1985), pp. 8–12. The

works by these authors are examined more fully in my newly published study; see Luke I. Johnson, *The Real Jesus: The Misguided Quest of the Historical Jesus and the Truth of the Traditional Gospels* (San Francisco: HarperSanFrancisco, 1995).

17 Meier, *Marginal Jew*, vol. 1, pp. 1–40.

18 See Robert A. Kraft and Gerhard Krodel (eds), *Orthodoxy and Heresy in Earliest Christianity* (Philadelphia: Fortress Press, 1971).

19 Morton Smith, *The Secret Gospel* (New York: Harper & Row, 1973).

20 Willi Marxsen, *Introduction to the New Testament*, trans. G. Buswell (Philadelphia: Fortress Press, 1968), pp. 59–68.

21 See, for example, A. De Oliveira, *Die Diakonie der Gerechtigheit und der Versöhnung in der Apologie des 2. Korintherbriefes* (Munster: Aschendorff, 1990), pp. 6–18.

22 For example, Raymond E. Brown, *The Community of the Beloved Disciple* (New York: Paulist Press, 1979).

23 Borg, *New Vision*, pp. 28–38. Geza Vermes's *Jesus the Jew* (New York: Macmillan, 1973), in fact, is also cited by A.N. Wilson and John Spong as a decisive influence. John Meier demonstrates just how little evidence there is on which to base such a 'type' (see *Marginal Jew*, vol. 2, pp. 583–90).

24 This becomes formulaic in Crossan's *Who Killed Jesus?* See, for example, pp. 11–12, 40–2, 50–8.

25 Mack, *Myth of Innocence*, p. 254.

26 See, for example, Crossan, *Historical Jesus*, p. 426; *Jesus: A Revolutionary Biography*, p. 200; and *Who Killed Jesus*, p. 217.

27 See Johnson, 'Crisis in Biblical Scholarship,' *Commonweal* 120 (April 1993), pp. 18–21, which agrees with many of the positions of Jon D. Levenson (*The Hebrew Bible, the Old Testament, and Historical Criticism* [Westminister: John Knox Press, 1993]).

28 It has taken me a long time to recognize the subtle influence on my thinking of Hans Frei, *The Identity of Jesus Christ. The Hermeneutical Bases of Dogmatic Theology* (Philadelphia: Fortress Press, 1975). In fact, even in the writing of my book (see note 16), I did not appreciate that I was moving back to a point made so well by Frei.

29 See, for example, the challenge to the image of Jesus as the suffering one in Michael Harrington. *The Vast Majority: A Journey to the World's Poor* (New York Simon & Shuster, 1977), pp. 94–5; or Susan Griffin, *Pornography and Silence* (New York: Harper & Row, 1981), pp. 14–15, 46–7, 68–9.

Chapter 19

Knowing Jesus through the Gospels

People called Christians profess that Jesus is present in the contemporary world, through the power of the Holy Spirit, more intimately and forcefully than during the short span of years before his death. This conviction is what distinguishes Christians from non-Christians, who all agree that Jesus has stayed dead. This difference in perspective dramatically affects people's answer to the question, 'What's the best way to learn Jesus?'

Jesus of Nazareth remains of compelling interest because of the ways in which he refuses to remain in the past as a crucified itinerant preacher of first-century Palestine. Some of the ways Jesus lives today are paralleled by other historical figures: he is the founding figure of a world religion, like Muhammad, for example, and has had even more literature devoted to his person and teachings than has Moses. But Muslims and Jews do not seriously consider Muhammad or Moses to be alive. Muslims and Jews agree with others who are not Muslims or Jews that Muhammad and Moses have stayed dead. The influence of these historical figures continues, but their personal stories are over.

In the case of Jesus, however, a significant portion of the world's population at this moment seriously shares the conviction that Jesus is alive now in a manner more substantial than through example or teaching.

THE CHRISTIAN CONVICTION

For those who consider Jesus as powerfully alive and present among his followers, Jesus can be learned in all the ways in which his presence is mediated: through the community of disciples, through worship, especially in the sacramental meal, through the saints whose lives have been shaped according to his image, through the little ones of the earth with whom Jesus promised to associate himself forever, and through the scriptures that speak of him in diverse and yet convergent ways. For people like these, learning Jesus is not a matter of scholarly research but of faithful discernment within communities of faith, not a matter of idiosyncratic inquiry but of truthful tradition, not a question of casual opinion but of passionate obedience. For such people, odd as they may seem to others, the writings of the New Testament are valuable precisely insofar as they testify to Jesus being the resurrected one. That is the Jesus whom their experience and conviction say is most real.

From the perspective of faith, the value of historical knowledge about Jesus is twofold. First, the convergence of evidence from both outsider and insider ancient sources provides the highest degree of historical probability that Jesus was a Jew of the first century who was executed under Roman authority. There is also a high degree of historical probability concerning other broad patterns in Jesus' ministry, such as his speaking in parables and associating with marginal elements in society. There is considerable historical probability that certain actions narrated in the Gospels happened, such as Jesus' baptism by John and his healing the sick.

This first function of historical knowledge enables believers to understand that their convictions concerning Jesus, although mythical in the sense that they ascribe divine power to a human being, are also basically attached to a person connected to world history in as certain a fashion as Julius Caesar.

A second reason why historical knowledge is important is that the writings that speak of Jesus in the New Testament do so from within a symbolic world that is both highly specific and massively different from our own. The more we know about the linguistics and social worlds of first-century Graeco-Roman culture and first-century Judaism, the better we are able to understand the witness to Jesus as a human person who lived and worked in those worlds, and is so portrayed in these writings. To ignore the bright light thrown on the New Testament by all the historical research of the past hundred years would be irresponsible, precisely because such knowledge expands and enhances our appreciation for the human Jesus discernible in its pages.

THE QUEST FOR THE HISTORICAL JESUS

Since the time of the Enlightenment, other people have argued for quite another use of history with respect to Jesus. Their position is that Jesus is best known by means of an historical reconstruction that eliminates the faith perspective of the New Testament compositions, and considers the gospel narratives, in particular, as requiring critical assessment as sources. Such a 'quest for the historical Jesus' can be undertaken from two distinct perspectives that, nevertheless, share the same historical premises and procedures. The first perspective is that of the believer in Jesus as the risen Lord who brackets that belief in order to engage Jesus as simply another deceased man of the past. This investigator does not think that the Church misrepresented Jesus in its tradition, but that there is, nonetheless, some value in securing what knowledge of Jesus is available to those who do not operate with the premise of faith. The second perspective is that of the person who thinks that the tradition, even beginning with the Gospels, got Jesus wrong. In this view, Jesus is not more powerfully alive than before, but is simply another dead man of the past; and there is no other legitimate way to comprehend him except through the same methods of historical research and recovery that gain us access to such figures as Julius Caesar.

Now, what is strange is that many people who approach Jesus this last way consider themselves to be Christian, at least in some broad sense. But they consider Jesus to be a person of historical significance only – as a teacher-prophet, for example – and not of eternal significance as the risen Son of God. Their Christianity is one that considers Christian tradition wrong about Jesus both in root and branch. The branches of development need to be pruned away, and the root of supernatural causality itself removed, before the simple historical Jesus can be seen – in his teaching, through his example – as the measure of authentic human life.

In this last case, the interest in historical reconstruction is actually theological more than historical. A reconstructed Jesus can and must, they insist, stand as a challenge to a distorted Christian faith, and save belivers from a deluded and destructive existence. It is clear that the ambition to find such a fully realized Jesus, who might serve this normative function, requires a con-siderably more sanguine view of history's potential with regard to Jesus than the few items I have earlier listed, for these are not more than a collection of facts. My reluctance to push further is based on a deep respect for proper historiographical method and the difficulties posed by these particular writings, considered as historical witnesses. First, their bias is intractable. The Gospels are not only written by believers. Belief in Jesus as the resurrected one suffuses everything recounted about him, and what is remem-bered of him is itself selected and shaped by communities who shared the same conviction.

The Gospels offer us no neutral evidence concerning Jesus. Even if we could cut away layer after layer of traditional accretion, we would still have only the earliest form of a tradition, not 'Jesus himself', but only the earliest available perception and interpretation of him (by a follower!). Second, the Gospels resist every question the historian poses. They give no basis for the reconstruction of a human life with its drama of psychological development. They offer at most three years of Jesus' ministry, but in so doing, report his sayings and deeds in different forms and sequences. They provide no access to Jesus' motivations and attitudes independent of the evangelists' interpretations of them. Undaunted by such difficulties, questers have leaped past the boundaries that say 'thus far and no farther' concerning Jesus. They have consistently followed the path of simplification by means of elimination and, by reaching a simple Jesus, they have mistakenly thought themselves to have gained a 'historical Jesus.'

A STRENUOUS EFFORT WITH NEGLIGIBLE RESULTS

The classic quest described by Albert Schweitzer in his 1906 *Quest of the Historical Jesus* began by eliminating the miraculous, then by eliminating John, then by eliminating Luke and Matthew as supposedly more 'theological' sources than the Gospel of Mark. When it was realized that Mark itself was by no means a straightforward historical narration about Jesus, but a complicated theological interpretation of him, the first quest came to an abrupt end.

The new quest has been encouraged by the mass of new material archaeological discoveries have made available, by new social-scientific models for dealing with history and, above all, by new methods of reading texts. The new materials do not, however, apart from the Coptic *Gospel of Thomas*, touch on Jesus himself in a significant way. The new models for history largely serve to provide frameworks into which the old fragmentary evidence can be fitted, and the new methods of reading texts turn out to be new ways of simplifying by elimination. Now, all the materials concerning Jesus are dissected in the effort to disentangle 'authentic Jesus sayings/deeds' from the influence of tradition. The small number of sayings and deeds that pass the test are (fallaciously) considered to be the bedrock Jesus material, which can then be fitted into a number of sociological stock-figures from antiquity. That's the mode of simplification followed by questers like J.D. Crossan and R. Funk. Another sort of simplification by elimination is followed by N.T. Wright, who tells a simple story of Jesus based on a selection of materials drawn from the Gospels and placed in the framework of an equally narrow version of Palestinian Judaism in the first century.

Coming up with a clear and cogent picture of Jesus is by no means the same thing as coming up with the historical Jesus. By pushing past the limits set by the evidence, both older and newer reconstructions of Jesus fail in their efforts to render a more adequate historical portrait of Jesus and, at the same time, distort the practice of history. The bewildering variety of Jesuses so confidently offered by diverse questers tends to discredit their claim that the disciplined application of scientific method has yielded the real Jesus, and makes even more dubious their proposal that such historical reconstructions should serve as the basis for a revised Christianity.

The gain from this strenuous effort, in short, is minimal and unreliable. The cost is more considerable. The premise that tradition distorted Jesus, and that it is necessary to get past tradition in order to reach Jesus, carries as its corollary the depreciation of the Gospel narratives. If the Gospels are historically inadequate, then they are inadequate in every respect: the real Jesus must be sought behind the texts rather than in the texts. Whether through a harmonizing 'pick and choose' method, or through a 'sifting all the materials for authenticity' method, the result is the same: the Gospels are considered valuable only as repositories of information about Jesus, and their specific interpretation of the humanity of Jesus is discarded.

Even in the most conservative reconstructions, Jesus stands apart as an abstraction from the earthy detail of the Gospel presentations. In effect, reconstructions invariably end up with something like the representation of Jesus in one of the Gospels at the cost of omitting the representation of him in the others. If the Jesus of Adolf Schlatter (writing in 1920) was an amalgam of Matthew and John, and paid the price of ignoring Mark and Luke, the Jesus of Crossan and Wright is found in Luke, but not in any of the other three canonical accounts. This is much too high a price to pay for such negligible results as those offered by the questers past and present.

THE GOSPELS: FOUR DISTINCT
NARRATIVE PORTRAITS

Another approach to knowing Jesus is available – even to those who do not consider Jesus as the risen Lord – that is far more satisfying, even historically. This is the reading of the Gospels as literary narratives precisely for the ways in which they diverge in their interpretations of Jesus, as well as for the ways that their witness tends to converge in certain important ways. Such reading does not seek to know Jesus through a reconstruction of him behind or beside the texts, but seeks to learn of him through engaging four distinct narrative portraits.

As readers through the ages and in all cultures have discovered, a very definite person emerges from these narratives, an identity that cannot be mistaken for any other ancient figure. The Jesus found within the Gospel narratives is not a transcendently powerful Lord but a deeply human figure, completely at home in the symbolic world of first-century Palestine. The application of literary-critical methods to these narratives only enhances them by revealing how intricate and purposeful their interpretations are, thereby also rendering their points of convergence concerning Jesus' character, portrayed in terms of obedience toward God and loving service to others, all the more impressive.

Reading the Gospels this way means giving up the attempt to reconstruct Jesus in a singular, simple, and completely self-consistent fashion, but that loss is trivial. What is gained are the literary and religious riches of narratives whose power to communicate an identity and to invite commitment is universally recognized. But such reading also gains access to a more adequate Jesus of history in two ways. First, the Gospels show Jesus as he was actually perceived and received by his followers in the aftermath of his resurrection. Thus they provide to later readers access to the historic Jesus, who so fundamentally shaped the course of history through this perception and reception. Second, the Gospels ground Jesus in the unmistakable and irreplaceable details of life in first-century Palestine. It remains the case that without the Gospels, our knowledge of Judaism in the first century would be greatly impoverished. And it stands as a remarkable fact that none of the new information about that world that we have gained through archaeology controverts any aspect of the portrayal of Jew or Greek in the Gospels. The tendency of such new discoveries has been, rather, to confirm the details of the Gospel narratives. In short, while the Gospels do not allow a satisfying reconstruction of Jesus' ministry, they do provide deeply satisfying access to Jesus' world.

The quest for the historical Jesus has never been about history. It has been about theology. In its attempt to find a Jesus behind the sources, the quest has paradoxically discredited the only sources that provide access to the human Jesus who worked among his people in the first century. Returning to an appreciative reading of the Gospels as narratives that witness and interpret that human Jesus, contemporary readers find not only a literary rendering of his identity, but as much history concerning Jesus as it is possible to acquire.

Chapter 20

Learning Jesus in Liturgy

I propose a way of knowing Jesus other than through historical reconstruction, namely, through Church liturgy. My problems with the variety of quests for the historical Jesus is well-documented (see *The Real Jesus: The Misguided Quest for the Historical Jesus and the Truth of the Traditional Gospels* (HarperSanFrancisco, 1996) and need only brief summarizing here.

First, the status of our sources does not allow the sort of full reconstruction that would enable us with a high degree of probability to say, 'This was Jesus' messianic project.' Second, the effort to push beyond the limits of responsible historiography ends up distorting good historical method and producing a Jesus who mirrors the ideal self of the questers in each generation. Third, such efforts distort historiography further by assuming its normativity – as though the determination of 'what really happened' in the past would ever matter apart from the contemporary decisions of communities about their past. Fourth, because historical reconstruction inevitably involves the dissecting or harmonizing of the Gospels, the rich and complex images of Jesus conveyed by those literary compositions as narratives are at least neglected and often rejected outright. Fifth, the effort to ground Christianity in a historical reconstruction of the human Jesus is theologically wrong-headed, because Christianity takes its stand on the good news that through the resurrection the human Jesus now shares God's own life, so that the 'real Jesus' in the ontological sense is, for Christians, not a dead man of the past, but a powerfully living Lord in the present.

As I try to show in my most recent book on the subject (*Living Jesus: Learning the Heart of the Gospel* (HarperSanFrancisco, 1999), an alternative to this dreary series of pseudoscientific quests is available. All that is required is taking the witness of the New Testament about the resurrection seriously, the willingness to consider faith as a genuine mode of human cognition, and participation in the worship life of a community that is still recognizably Christian.

The New Testament does not speak of Jesus' resurrection as a resuscitation but as a new creation, not an historical but an eschatological event. The defining event of Christian existence escapes historical detection because it transcends the capacity of historical categories to contain it. Jesus, says Paul, has become 'life-giving Spirit', which is to say that he shares the very life of God. The symbol of Jesus' new way of being is his glorified body. That Jesus is resurrected bodily means that it really is the human Jesus who lives, not some vague and impersonal world-spirit; the resurrected Jesus who appears at the disciples' meals is continuous with the Jesus who ate with them before his death. But that Jesus' body is *glorified* means that Jesus is now more than human, indeed shares God's own power and life. He is no longer confined to the empirical, historical body that was his before his death, but can as Spirit enter the bodies of others. This is precisely what is meant by Paul when he speaks of Christ being 'in us' and we being 'in Christ', and when he speaks of the Church as the 'Body of the Christ'. This is not for Paul – or for the classic Christian tradition – a nice metaphor. It is a symbol, a bodily representation, of spiritual reality.

If the resurrected one is life-giving Spirit and can intimately and internally touch all the bodies of the earth, then the ways of knowing the living Jesus instantly become remarkably rich and complex. Jesus can be encountered and learned within the body of disciples with whom he has chosen to associate. Christians value Jesus' declaration, 'Where two or three are gathered in my name, there am I in their midst,' not because Jesus necessarily said it in the past, but because it speaks truth about the resurrected and living Jesus in the present. Jesus can also be learned in and through the saints, those humans whose lives have been transformed into the image of Christ through the power of the Holy Spirit. In their variety in expression and consistency in character, saints remind us of the multiple ways the same 'mind of Christ' (1 Cor. 2:16) can be embodied in the world. Finally, Jesus can be met and learned through all the 'little ones of the earth', the children and the poor and the marginal and the outcast, with whom in particular he associated himself (see Matt. 25). Receiving the stranger in hospitality, visiting the sick and imprisoned, feeding and clothing the poor, these are not for the Christian a matter of *noblesse oblige*; they are an opportunity to see the embodied face of Christ and learn how Jesus continues to visit the earth and call humans to faith and love.

If all this is true – and the entire history of Christianity insists that it is – then the liturgy of the Church is a preeminent locus for learning Jesus. It is not a seminar for studying the historical past of Jesus. It is a place where the living Jesus is engaged through the assembly that is a chief embodiment of his presence in the world. The church becomes Church in the fullest sense when it gathers in the name of Jesus and when, filled with the power of his Holy Spirit, it practises prayer and reading and preaching and the meal. In the Church's liturgy, everything that is meant positively by 'tradition' comes into play: the liturgy brings to expression the convictions and practices of the living community across time in conversation with its living Lord. And if tradition can and does obscure dimensions of the truth about Jesus – tradition certainly needs critical assessment if it is to remain creatively loyal to the one in whose name it exists – tradition nevertheless has to do with a living presence and not a reconstituted historical figure.

Notice what a fundamental epistemological decision is involved by seeking to learn Jesus in the context of the Church's worship. Since the time of the Enlightenment, religion's cultured despisers have rejected faith as a legitimate mode of human understanding, insisting that only empirical knowledge counts. In the case of Jesus, the various questers who represent the last hurrah of modernity insist that the Church's tradition must be measured by the results of historical research: if historians could show that Jesus did not claim to be the Messiah, Christians are wrong to consider him so; if Jesus did not think of himself as God's child, then Christians are mistaken when they so declare him. In effect, this stance nullifies the knowledge of Jesus that comes from the experience of him today within the life of the Church. Against such epistemological monism, faith insists on taking its stand not on empirical research but on existential reality. And by opening the eyes of faith to the ways in which Jesus makes himself known in today's world, faith insists that such learning is not only legitimate but indispensable. It begins by trusting that the Jesus who speaks and acts within the liturgy is real and finds that trust confirmed by the experience of an enriched reality.

The risen Jesus can be learned in and through the liturgical assembly itself, for in that 'Body of Christ' the face of Jesus can be discerned in multiple forms. Each community contains not only those whose lives are being transformed by the Spirit of Jesus but also those who represent the little ones of the earth. The voice of Jesus can be spoken by each and heard by each. The presence of the risen Jesus in the assembly means that Christians must cultivate gifts of speaking and hearing alike. Not only in the formal expressions of the cult, but in all the verbal conversation and mute body language of the congregation, Jesus can be learned – if the eyes and ears of faith are open.

For communities that have a strong sense of sacrament, it is above all the presence of Jesus in the Eucharist that enables a learning of Jesus that is both spiritual and embodied. The Eucharist is the supreme example of how the glorious body of the risen Lord both transcends and is immanent within the body of the believing community, the way in which believers 'recognize him' in the gestures of breaking and blessing (Luke 24:31) as he makes himself 'known to them in the breaking of the bread' (Luke 24:35). The celebration of Jesus' presence in the Lord's

Supper is the Church's most consistent ritual witness to the reality of the resurrection.

The learning of Jesus in the Eucharist is profound because it is communal, because it is ritualized, and because it involves the magic of the common meal. The community that is marked by the sign of the cross in its baptism and understands itself to be a paschal, that is, a dying and rising community, now hears in its shared meal, where Jesus is present in the Spirit, the words of Jesus over the bread and the wine that define his existence as one of life given away so that others might live: 'This is my body, the one that is for you. . . . This is the cup that is the new covenant in my blood' (1 Cor. 11:24–25).

The Church that not only hears these words every week but also eats that bread and drinks that wine enters into a mode of exchange, a way of knowing, that resembles imprinting more than it does information. The Church 'drinks of one Spirit' (1 Cor. 12:12) and becomes the 'Body of Christ' (1 Cor. 12:27). And what does the Church thereby learn? It learns 'the mind of Christ' (1 Cor. 2:16) as expressed in the bodily self-disposition of Christ, and learns 'this mind that was in Christ Jesus' that it is to have within it as well, by living in mutual service and upbuilding (Phil. 2:5–11). The community is thus reminded that any self-aggrandizing behaviour that destroys or even diminishes others absolutely contradicts the pattern of life learned in this meal. Week after week, the community that gathers itself in this name and gathers into itself this food and story finds itself shaped by a vision of the world that consists in the profoundest service of the world. And that is to *learn Jesus*.

The worshipping community also learns Jesus through the reading of Scripture and preaching, through modes of prophecy and prayer. The reading of Scripture itself creates a complex conversation concerning Jesus – or better, witnessing to the reality of the living Jesus – within the liturgical assembly. The Church not only reads aloud Gospel passages and Epistles that speak explicitly about Jesus past and present and to come, but joins these to readings from Torah and the responsorial singing of the Psalms.

The Gospel passages about Jesus are given new contexts consisting of these other narratives and prophecies and writings addressed first to Israel and then to the Church of the first generation. Those hearing these texts are invited to construct, in an almost kalaeidoscopic manner, images of Jesus with shifting dimensions and aspects. The Jesus story echoes or answers the texts of Torah; the words of the Psalms can be sung as the words of Jesus himself as well as the words of Israel and the Church; the Epistles establish angles of intersection and tangent with the story of Jesus. All these intertextual connections interact with the complex ways in which the living Jesus is experienced by those speaking and hearing in the assembly, creating a sense of Jesus within the imagination that transcends literal or univocal reduction.

Preaching in the assembly actualizes the texts of Scripture by explicitly connecting them to the situation and experiences of contemporary believers. People's understanding of Jesus is deepened and given new dimensions by the ways in which the stories of the past and the many stories of the present are brought into conversation by the act of preaching. The readers and preachers of the texts bear witness to Jesus as foreshadowed in Torah and the Prophets, as sung in the Psalms, as speaking and acting in the Gospels, as interpreted in the Letters, and as experienced in the world today.

Words of prophecy also speak with the Spirit and voice of the living Jesus. In some traditions – such as the Pentecostal – the ancient modes of prophetic speech (in tongues and in intelligible speech) continue to be active. But there are other modes of prophecy as well. Preaching at its best is an obvious example; for at its best it can do what Paul said of prophetic discourse: one hearing it can have the heart convicted and declare, 'God is in the midst of you' (1 Cor. 14:25). But there are also all the forms of witnessing, storytelling, advocacy and protest that the Church allows itself to hear as it seeks the presence and the call of the living God. The Book of Revelation portrays the risen Jesus speaking in such a voice of prophecy to the real-life churches of Asia in the first century (Revelation 2–3). The Church continues to be a place where prophecy can be spoken in the name of Jesus.

Christians learn Jesus through prayer. Some forms of prayer are liturgical. Paul's community in Corinth addressed Jesus when they prayed, 'Maranatha, our Lord, come!' (1 Cor. 16:22). Paul spoke for all when he declared that because Jesus is the 'yes to all God's promises', so also we say 'Amen to God through him' (2 Cor. 1:20). The Acts of the Apostles describes a particularly powerful example of liturgical prayer: After the persecution of the apostles they gather and pray:

> 'And now Lord, look upon their threats and grant to thy servants to speak thy word with all boldness, while thou stretchest out thy hand to heal, and signs and wonders are performed through the name of thy Holy Servant Jesus.' And when they had prayed, the place in which they were gathered together was shaken; and they were all filled with the Holy Spirit and spoke the word of God with boldness.
>
> (Acts 4:31 RSV)

Less dramatically than this, but no less powerfully, Christians through the ages have experienced the powerful presence of Jesus in the Holy Spirit when at gathered prayer. Such prayer is not always or necessarily spoken aloud. Indeed, some of the most powerful experiences of Jesus' presence have occurred in those spaces of silence within worship when the word is allowed to gather and come to a point in the hearts of the believers.

In the liturgy of the Church, the living Jesus is learned in multiple and complex ways. It is a real knowledge, for the minds and hearts of those learning are changed in fundamental ways through participation in the Eucharist and reading and preaching and prophecy and prayer. It is a real knowledge of Jesus, for he is the one spoken of by the texts, he is the one proclaimed, he is the one addressed in prayer, he is the one heard in prophecy. It is a knowledge that is never-ending and always complex, for it responds to a living presence and invites learning from many sources. It is a knowledge that always contains elements of ambiguity, precisely because it is the epistemology of faith, which

175

refuses to reduce what is essentially mysterious to the level of a problem.

Is this a scholarly or scientific knowledge? Of course not. Knowing *persons* is not the same thing as knowing facts or learning theories. This is the sort of knowledge, rather, that human persons experience when they give themselves to each other in trust and loyalty over time. Is it a knowledge that can be disconfirmed? Yes, for a life lacking in the transformative power of the resurrection, a life devoid of self-donative service to other humans, would strongly suggest that whatever was learned in the assembly, it was *not* Jesus.

Is this a learning of Jesus, finally, that is true to the Scriptures? I hold that it is, not only because the liturgy itself breathes the words of Scripture in each of its parts, but because it was for the liturgical assembly that the Scriptures were first written and where they were first read. It was by people within such communities of worship and prayer that the narratives about Jesus were first com-posed on the basis of shared memories. There exists a perfect fit between the Gospels and the liturgy based on the fact that they speak of the same Jesus. Each in its way and each together bears witness to Jesus, not as a dead person of the past, but as a powerful person in the present. The very thing about the Gospels that is the biggest obstacle to the questers after the historical Jesus – namely, their resurrection perspective – is the very aspect that makes them most valuable to believers and most true to their experience of the living Jesus.

Contrary to some claims, the knowledge of Jesus gained through the liturgy, above all through the reading of Scripture in the context of the sacramental meal, is not abstract and detached. It is as specific and embodied as those gathered in his name, far more specific than those sociological types that pass for historical Jesuses. Through the power of the risen one, believers are pro-gressively shaped according to the pattern of life found uniquely and unmistakably in the human Jesus: a life of radical obedience to God and of self-sacrificing service to others. The liturgy is a practice that shapes and expresses the learning that is discipleship.

Chapter 21

The Eucharist and the Identity of Jesus

The Gospels do not encourage the objective form of knowing that allows distance and detachment, but demand that deeply subjective form of learning that requires risk and intimacy. The point of reading the Gospels is not to know about Jesus but rather to learn Jesus as does a disciple, that is, to be transformed into the very identity we discover in our reading. The faithful reading of the Gospels does not ask, 'What really happened?' but asks instead, 'Who is this who speaks and acts now in my life? How can I learn him in my present from this witness and interpretation of his past as read by those who first experienced him also as present to them after his death?'

When truth of this sort is sought, there is no end of learning. The most powerful argument to be made for the divine inspiration of the Gospels is that there is no end of learning for those who read them. Although the Gospels yield their surface stories readily to the most casual visitor, they keep giving endlessly to those who inhabit them.

It is in this conviction that I turn to one of the best known and loved Gospel stories, the passage in Luke that tells of the encounter between two disciples and the risen Jesus on the road to Emmaus, as a starting point for thinking about the identity of Jesus Christ in the Eucharist (Luke 24: 13–35). Jesus appears as a stranger to Cleopas and another disciple as they make that afternoon walk from Jerusalem, speaks with them on the road about the events concerning himself, interprets Moses and all the prophets in light of his death and resurrection, breaks bread with them, and then vanishes. For many, it is the most beautiful of resurrection stories, the more powerfully evocative for the simplicity and apparent artlessness of its narration. For some of us, the story is even more overlaid with resonance because of the practice of prayer: the plaintive plea in the divine office, *mane nobiscum domine, quoniam advesperascit*, 'stay with us Lord, for it has become evening', is drawn from the words of the disciples as they invite Jesus to share their meal, and gains even more poignancy as those who still remember the Latin move into the evening of their lives.

BREAKING OF THE BREAD

I focus on the single line concluding the passage: 'They related what had happened on the road, and how they recognized him in the breaking of the bread' (Luke 24:35). More literally, we can translate, 'how he became known to them in the breaking of the bread'. This summary statement echoes and points the reader back to the climax of the story: 'While he was reclining at table with them, Jesus took bread. He broke it and blessed it. He gave it to them. They recognized him.' Here, Luke uses the verb *epiginoskein*, 'to come to a recognition'. We are to understand this, then, as a recognition story, a narrative about learning Jesus.

To grasp the significance of this recognition, we need to ponder two puzzles. The first is why they should not have known that they were with Jesus all along. The second is why their recognition came at the moment when he broke bread and blessed it and gave it to them.

Think for a moment how odd it is that these two people in particular should encounter Jesus on their journey and yet fail to know him. Luke explicitly identifies them, after all, as being from 'among them' (24:13). When they speak of Jesus (to Jesus!) they associate themselves not with the chief priests and leaders who had put him to death, but with Jesus' followers: they regarded him as a 'prophet mighty in deed and in speech' (24:20), and declare that 'we had hoped that he was the very one who was going to liberate Israel' (24:21). These are not the observers of the events in Jerusalem, but participants. We are to understand them as among those who had followed Jesus from Galilee, and at his crucifixion, 'stood a long way off' (23:49). These were followers of Jesus, moreover, who had heard news of his resurrection, if in a confused form. They know of the visit of the women to the tomb and their report of a missing body and that they had seen messengers (or angels) there (24:23). They were followers, they were devoted, they had heard of his resurrection. But they were nevertheless in a state of despair. We had hoped, they say, not, 'we are hoping'.

DIVINE ACTION

Why should such as these not recognize 'Jesus himself' (as the narrator calls him in 24:15) when he joins them in their conversation? We could speculate about the physical appearance of Jesus, or the psychological condition of the disciples. Luke simply tells us, 'they were prevented from recognizing him'. The Greek reads literally, 'their eyes were held in order that they might not recognize him'. Two things about this construction are striking. The first is that this was not something in their control; the passive voice suggests a divine action. The second is the purposefulness of the prevention, as though the narrator wanted us to see that something was lacking in them that only their further experience would repair.

Our second puzzle is why they should suddenly recognize Jesus in the act of breaking, blessing, and sharing bread. Are not these gestures that accompany every meal in Judaism? Why should they remind them particularly of Jesus? At this point, we should pay some attention to the story just preceding this one, Luke's version of the empty-tomb story (24:1–11). It is quite different in several respects from the accounts in Matthew and Mark. Most distinctive is the message of the men to the women. They are not told to go and tell the disciples that Jesus goes before them to Galilee. Instead, they are turned backward to the memory of Galilee.

They are told, 'Remember how he spoke to you while he was still in Galilee. He said, "the Son of Man must be handed over into the hand of people who are sinners, be crucified, and on the third day rise." ' And Luke tells us that the women remembered his words (Luke 24:7–8).

For Luke, it seems, the recognition of Jesus as the risen one ('Why do you seek the living one among the dead? He is not here but has been raised,' Luke 24:5–6) is intimately connected to the memory of the words that he spoke. Does Luke in our passage suggest something similar about Jesus' *actions*, so that the recognition of his presence as the living one might also demand the memory of his character as revealed in his bodily gestures during his life?

THE FREEDOM OF JESUS

Taking our lead from Luke, then, we can also 'remember Galilee', by observing Jesus in Luke's own narrative, paying particular attention to what Jesus does, seeking to discover how the disciples came to recognize him in the breaking of the bread. As I follow Jesus through Luke's narrative, observing him as a character moving among other characters, I am struck most of all by his remarkable freedom. This sounds paradoxical, for Jesus also appears to be someone whose destiny is determined both by a script provided by Scripture and by the will of powers over which he has no control. Even in the course of his ministry, Jesus seems to make few real choices. He mostly seems to respond to what presents itself to him.

But perhaps here is exactly where we find his freedom. Jesus is so defined by his faithful obedience to God that he is free to be available to whatever presents itself. Nowhere in ancient literature do we find an equally accessible character. Jesus is approached by everyone, friend and enemy, lowly and powerful, and most of all by the needy, who seem to know intuitively that he can be so approached. And Jesus receives them all. He is immediately present to them all. Jesus is never distracted. Nowhere – except for those moments when he retreats for prayer – does Jesus give the slightest sense that there is something more important to do than what he is then doing.

Because he refuses to be defined by any finite plan or project, he is not enslaved by any finite plan or project. Because he is defined by the God who transcends all, because his project is only to respond to the project of God who chooses – who knows why? – to work out that project moment by moment, Jesus is free to be available to all others in their projects and plans, without being defined by them, either. In his being present to every moment given to him by God – with every moment's pleasure and every moment's pain – Jesus is perfectly faithful and fully free.

And by his freedom, he liberates those he encounters. Just as it is remarkable how accessible Jesus is, it is equally remarkable that Jesus does not enter intrusively into the lives of those he encounters. He visits their houses but does not become part of their family. He remains in a very real sense the stranger, even as he gains astonishing intimacy. He is present to them, it appears, in order that they might be more truly present to themselves. The story of Jesus' visit with Martha and Mary (Luke 10:38–42) is the perfect example. He is 'at home' with them, fully aware and attentive. Yet we can feel him leaving even as he arrives. And his presence serves to reveal the truth of their presence to each other (in all its complexity) and thereby to reveal the possibility of a fuller presence to each other because of the (almost accidental) presence of the one who is leaving even as he sits there.

Ancient writers were correct in understanding Jesus' parable of the Samaritan (Luke 10:25–37) as self-referential (see Origen, *Homilies on Luke* 34). The Samaritan who risks everything to help the stricken Jewish traveller, who binds his wounds, pays for his lodging, promises to return to settle any further debt, then leaves, to continue his own journey. The injured man is healed because of the touch of the stranger. But the stranger enters the injured man's life only to restore it, not to replace it with his own patronage.

PHYSICAL GESTURES

Catching a glimpse of the freedom of Jesus that liberates is not irrelevant to our search for what Jesus does with his hands. His physical gestures express the freedom that liberates. Notice now Jesus is accessible to the touch of others: the people afflicted with unclean spirits throng around him and touch him (Luke 6:19), and they are freed of their affliction; the sinful woman touches Jesus in an intimate and public fashion as an expression of her love, and much is forgiven her because she loves much (7:36–50). The woman who had suffered for years with bleeding touches him with faith, and she is healed (8:44–46). They touch Jesus, and they are changed.

But Jesus also touches. When, at the beginning of his ministry, the sick crowd about them, 'he placed his hands on each one of them' (4:40). When approached by a man with leprosy, he 'reached out his hand and touched him' (5:13). Coming upon the woman of Nain who was mourning her recently dead son, Jesus touches the bier on which the young man is placed, and when the young man comes back to life, Jesus 'gave him to his mother' (7:15). When called to the bedside of the little girl who has died, Jesus takes her hands and commands her to rise, and when she gets up, commands that she be given something to eat (8:54–55). Jesus heals the epileptic child when his disciples are not able to, and then 'gave him to his father' (9:42). Jesus takes hold of a little child and places him beside himself to teach his disciples about greatness in the Kingdom (9:47), just as he receives the little children when his disciples try to turn them away and declares that the Kingdom is made up of such as them (18:15–17). Jesus places his hands on the woman in the synagogue and liberates her to stand upright (13:13). When he is at table in the house of a Pharisee and a man with dropsy appears, Jesus takes hold of the man and heals him and then releases him (14:4). Finally, in the last free act of his career, at the moment of his arrest leading to his death, Jesus touches the man whose ear Peter has sliced off, and heals him (22:51).

What does Jesus do with his hands in Luke's gospel? He does not seize, he does not control, he does not force. He reaches out and touches that which is broken and makes it well. Through his touch he restores people who are alienated by demonic possession, impurity, disease and even death, to themselves and to the possibility of human community. Twice, in the case of children either dead or on the verge of death, we read that Jesus 'gives them' to their parents. In that touch, in that gesture of giving, I think, one can recognize the essential character of Jesus.

SHARING MEALS

Luke's gospel also shows Jesus frequently at meals. Once more we can see his accessibility. He shares meals with tax-collectors and sinners (5:27–39) and in fact has a reputation for preferring such table-fellowship (7:34; 15:1–2). But he also shares meals with the religiously righteous Pharisees who consistently oppose him – even in the context of the meal (11:37–54; 14:1). It is at such a meal, in the house of the Pharisee Simon, that Jesus is shown such extravagant hospitality by the sinful woman (7:36–50).

Three meals in particular, however, help us understand why the disciples on the road to Emmaus were able to recognize Jesus in the breaking of the bread. The first is hardly a meal at all. It happens as Jesus is travelling on the Sabbath with his followers early in his ministry (6:1–5). They are hungry. They pass through grain fields. It is the Sabbath. The disciples gather a snack as they move through the fields. When the Pharisees attack Jesus for breaking Sabbath, Jesus responds by appealing to the example of David and his companions. Luke's choice of words is intriguing: 'Have you not even read what David did when he and his companions were hungry? He entered the house of God, took the presentation loaves that only the priests were allowed to eat, ate them, and gave some to his companions. The Son of Man is Lord of the Sabbath' (6:4–5). We could spend much time thinking about this passage in light of Jesus' astonishing freedom with regard to himself and his companions, with regard to the Sabbath and the interpretation of Scripture. But the story wonderfully captures the sense of Jesus' freedom as directed by the occasion God presents: specifically, the very human necessity to eat when hungry and the legitimacy of meeting that basic need despite religious constraints. And most striking is the language Luke chooses: he has David 'take the loaves' and 'eat' and 'give to his companions'.

FEEDING THE FIVE THOUSAND

The second meal involving his disciples is the open-air feeding of the five thousand in a deserted place (9:11–17). In Luke, the story occurs in the context of Jesus' project of sending out and instructing his disciples as agents of his mission of proclaiming the Kingdom of God and healing. When they return with the good news of their success, Luke deliberately notes the continuity between Jesus' work and theirs by relating how Jesus welcomed the great crowd that had followed him, spoke to them concerning the Kingdom of God, and those having need of healing he cured (9:11). Jesus then feeds the crowd because they are hungry and because they are in a deserted place. Luke clearly intends his readers to see that this great meal, enabled by Jesus' miraculous power to multiply five loaves of bread and two fishes into a meal that has leftovers that can be collected in twelve baskets (9:17), is continuous with Jesus' self-emptying service to the people in his teaching and healing. It is another way in which his hands touch them. But now, he involves the twelve in the feeding, just as he had associated them with his teaching and healing. So Jesus takes the five loaves of bread and two fish. He looks up to heaven. He blesses and breaks them. And then, 'he gave them to the disciples to serve the crowd' (9:16). The common meal expresses the reality of the common life. The common life is defined by the teaching of the Kingdom and the restoration of the people. Authority within the community consists in teaching and healing. These realities are symbolized by the meal in which those who teach and heal also wait on tables and serve food to those they teach and heal.

The third meal shared by Jesus and his disciples in Luke's narrative is the Passover meal before his betrayal, arrest, trial and execution (22:14–23). Already powerful in its own right as the celebration of God's liberation of the people in the Exodus, and as Jesus' farewell meal, sealed with his prophetic utterance, 'I will not eat it until the time when it is fulfilled in the kingdom of God', the scene takes on even deeper meaning when read as the climax of Jesus' time among the people as one who touched and healed and fed the multitude. Now, when Jesus takes bread and gives thanks, and breaks it and gives it to them – the same words in the same sequence as in the feeding of the multitude – his interpretive words make plain that his hands express his essential body language: 'This is my body, which is being given for you.' And when he hands them the wine, 'This cup is the new covenant in my blood which is being poured out for you' (22:19–20). Just as the bread and fishes at the feeding symbolized Jesus' ministry of service in teaching and healing, so the bread and wine symbolize the death that perfectly and finally expresses his identity as God's gift of love in service to humanity. His body – that is, his very self – is being given for them. It was given through ministry, it shortly will be given as he is 'handed over' to the death he had so frequently predicted. His blood – that is, his very life – is being poured out for them.

VISION OF AUTHORITY

Two further aspects of Luke's depiction of the Last Supper are of particular importance to our reflection, not least because they are distinctive to his Gospel. The first is the instruction on authority among the disciples that follows his self-donative gesture at the meal. In response to their competitive argument about who is the greatest among them – at this moment! – Jesus presents a new vision of authority. It is not to consist in domination over others, but is to be expressed by littleness and service: 'The greater among you is to become as the younger. And the one who governs is to be as one who serves.' This radical vision of authority is now spelled out, so characteristically, in terms of the dynamics of a meal: 'For who is greater, the one who reclines at table, or the one who serves at table?' The answer is obvious to anyone in the Hellenistic world or in our world of five-star restaurants, and Jesus supplies it: 'Is it not the one who reclines at table?' This is the way of the world. But what is the way of Jesus? He continues, 'But I am in your midst as the one who serves at table' (Luke 23:24–27).

The lesson could not be plainer: those who continue Jesus' authority in the Kingdom must do so through such radical and self-emptying service. Just as surely as Judas' betrayal of his discipleship was expressed at the meal, when Jesus says, 'Look, the hand of the one betraying me is with me on the table' (23:21), is the betrayal of the other disciples' authority expressed through their rivalrous contentions at the meal. The common meal will henceforth be a place that reveals the identity of Jesus and the integrity of those who serve him. The identity of Jesus is expressed through self-giving service to others; the integrity of leadership is revealed through servanthood.

Luke has one final distinctive note to this account. After Luke has Jesus declare over the bread, 'This is my body which is being given for you,' he adds the words, 'Keep doing this as a remembrance of me' (22:19). As it happens, Paul also remembers Jesus' words in this same form, when he reminds the Corinthians of Jesus' last meal: 'This is my body, the one for you. Keep on doing this in my remembrance' (1 Cor 11:24). Both Paul and Luke have 'keep doing *touto*', that is, 'this thing'. But what does Jesus mean by 'this thing'? Does it mean the ritual of breaking bread in his name? Yes, surely that. But surely also more than that. Surely Jesus means by 'this thing' all that his gesture of breaking bread as his body and pouring out wine as his blood signifies as the gift of his life given in service to humanity. Keeping on doing this thing means, therefore, not only celebrating a ritual but above all living according to this pattern. This gesture, with this meaning, reveals the identity of Jesus in the Church. And this is, as Jesus says, the 'remembrance of me'.

MEALS IN CONTEXT

We have come full circle back to our starting passage. We have noted that the women at the tomb were told to 'remember' what Jesus had said, and, applying that advice to his actions as well, we have sought to remember those characteristic gestures of Jesus in the Gospel that reveal his identity. In his acts of healing and in the meals he shared with others, we have found such gestures, and now are able to understand how the disciples walking to Emmaus, whose eyes were held from recognition, were jolted into memory when they saw Jesus break bread before them, heard him bless God, and felt his touch as he handed the bread to them. But as in the other passages we have thought about, the action of the meal was given context by the other ways Jesus was present with them on their journey. He joined them on their walk as a stranger. He listened to their story of early hope, recent despair, and ambiguous rumour. And then, as always, Jesus placed himself at their service. As he had always done before, now he does with an unparalleled explicitness. First, he jolts them with a rebuke. They are without understanding. And the reason is that their hearts are slow to believe. The problem, in other words, is not their minds but their affections, their will. They do not want to acknowledge what Jesus had told them time and again, that it was necessary for the Messiah to suffer these things and enter into glory. But if they could not grasp the very essence of what it meant when Jesus broke bread as his body and poured out wine as his blood, if they could not admit into their hearts the mystery of suffering that is the identity of the one God sent to bear the world's sins, then how could they recognize the face of the resurrected one in any of its guises?

So as the resurrected one who has himself passed through that terrible suffering, Jesus teaches them once more, now more powerfully and unforgetably: 'beginning from Moses and all the prophets, he interpreted for them the things concerning himself in all the scriptures' (24:27). It is the resurrected Lord who teaches them how to read both Scripture and their experience of Jesus himself. They understand what it means for him to be the suffering Messiah because they read him in the light of the twice-rejected Moses and the suffering servant Isaiah and the righteous suffering one of the Psalms. And they come to understand the true meaning of the law and the prophets because of what they have experienced of God's work in Jesus.

TRANSFORMED

Having taught them, Jesus is ready to move again into the evening shadow, but Luke the narrator is no more ready to have him depart than are the disciples who beg him to remain with them, and then, in the breaking of the bread, recognize him for who he truly is. And with that recognition, Jesus does disappear. His presence has been to make their presence to each other more real and powerful than it could be before. So the disciples now say to each other, 'Were our hearts not burning within us as he spoke to us on the road, as he opened the scripture to us?' Now that they recognize Jesus in the breaking of the bread, they are able also to rightly interpret their earlier experience: in the stranger who opened their hearts to the Scripture they also encountered Jesus. They know this: because their hearts burned within them. They are transformed by the presence of Jesus and the opening of the Scripture. And their response? They return to the others, share their good news with them, and hear in turn the story of how Jesus had appeared to Simon. In such separate experiences and shared stories, the Church comes into existence. Through such encounters with saints and strangers, through such openings of Scripture, and through such breakings of bread, the Church remains in existence as the body of the risen Messiah.

We cannot read passages like this one too often or too slowly, for in reading the story of the first disciples, we read and come to understand our own story as well. We are called to acknowledge the ways in which we lack understanding and are slow to believe in the presence of the risen one. We are challenged because of our reluctance to face the suffering that lies at the heart of the good news and therefore in our personal transformation. We are rebuked for the ways in which we seek not to serve but to be served. We are reminded that as for us so also for the very first believers, the Church was a fragile web of experience and story and Scripture. We are encouraged to open our eyes to the strangers who might join us unrecognized on our journey, to open our eyes to the Scriptures that shape our world and, always, to the breaking of the bread in which the identity of our dear Saviour is revealed.

Chapter 22

How Does Jesus Save Us?

Christians have never had a hard time calling Jesus Saviour, but they have had a hard time agreeing on what that designation means. They have debated not only how Jesus saves but also whom he saves, and from what. The understanding of Jesus as Saviour, in other words, involves a more comprehensive construal of the human situation. One understanding of salvation is deeply rooted in the New Testament and in the Catholic tradition. That understanding, however, has faced severe challenge from two fronts, one ancient and one modern. Each claims a basis in the New Testament, but each is actually driven by an understanding of the human situation at odds with that found in the Bible.

SALVATION IN GNOSTICISM

In the second century, the version of Christianity called Gnosticism focused on the salvation of the individual soul from the body. The soul needed saving since it had fallen into the body by mistake or malevolence. In this system, only spirit is good. Materiality is evil. The spirit within humans, in fact, was a spark of the divine being that had become imprisoned in the flesh. It could be saved by being awakened, brought to knowledge of its true being, and liberated from the shackles of the flesh. Gnostics saw Christ as another spark of the divine light who came to proclaim the good news of individual liberation, which was that those who were already from the light could return through true knowledge back to the light – no surprise that the Gnostics liked the Gospel of John best, even if they did not read all of it carefully! Necessarily, then, the Christ was divine spirit, no less than the divine spirits he was sent to gather back to the light. But the role of Jesus in this system was ambiguous. The Christ-Aeon could be conceived of as using the human Jesus, but not as being incarnated, for the divine goodness could not be associated with evil materiality. Gnosticism had little good to say about ordinary human life or about social institutions. It was entirely individualistic. The point of salvation was the return of the divine soul to its source. A community could only impede, not help, such salvation. And the human Jesus is no more than a cipher for the revelation by which the sparks of light could fly back to their source.

Gnosticism was explicitly rejected in the second century, but it lived on within the tradition in such heretical strains as Mono-physitism, which so emphasized the divine nature of Christ as almost to negate his humanity altogether. And the spirit of Gnos-ticism continues in those forms of Christian spirituality that con-cern themselves only with the salvation of the individual, with no care for the wider world at all.

SALVATION IN LIBERATION THEOLOGY

A second version of salvation is offered by contemporary Libera-tion Theologies. Now the human predicament is located not in the individual but in society. Sinful and alienating social structures keep humans from realizing their full potential. Patriarchalism, racism, imperialism, colonialism, ageism, speciesism – these are the systemic patterns of oppression and marginalization that engender and perpetuate the spiritual diseases of envy, competi-tion, rage, violence and murder. Salvation will be accomplished when the social order reflects 'the rule of God' preached by Jesus and exemplified by his style of life, when people live together in an egalitarian, classless, inclusive, multicultural and harmonious society. In this understanding of salvation, it is not quite clear how God saves, except through the efforts of humans who work for such a social agenda; nor is it clear how Jesus is Saviour, except as his proclamation of the good news in Nazareth (Luke 4:16–32) and his beatitudes (Luke 6:20–24) sketch the agenda, while his embrace of the outcast among his people suggested how it might be fulfilled.

If the Gnostic understanding focused completely on the salvation of the individual and had no regard for the social order, the Liberation understanding gives little attention to the transformation of the individual person. Hope for a future life with God, indeed, distracts from the essential work of establishing the rule of God here and now in visible fashion. Just as the Gnostic movement in the second century so appealed to the dualistic mood of the age that it seriously challenged the orthodox position, so in the late twentieth century Liberation Theology has made very substantial inroads into Christian consciousness, at least partly because the orthodox understanding of salvation has been viewed (to some extent correctly) as perpetuating an individualistic and socially irresponsible spirituality. The popularity of the Liberation perspective can be seen in many of the recent publications devoted to 'the Historical Jesus'. Jesus appears in these books primarily as the reformer of the social order, and the good news amounts to the vision of a society freed from every form of distinction and discrimination.

OVERSIMPLIFYING SALVATION

The fundamental problem with both these understandings of salvation is that they oversimplify. First, they oversimplify the situation humans need saving from. Escaping our bodies or changing our social structures will not address the real issue, which is disease of the human heart, that distortion of human freedom that we call sin. Second, they oversimplify the witness of scripture. Rather than deal with the complex witness of all the writings, each understanding begins with an ideological standpoint and selects the passages and themes that can be fitted to it. Third, they oversimplify the story of salvation by taking away its relational character. In Gnosticism, human freedom is denied from the start, for the soul is fated to be imprisoned in the body or liberated from it. In its purest form, indeed, Gnostic salvation is really God saving God, since the scattered spirits/sparks are essentially fallen from the source to which they are to return. In Liberation Theologies, human freedom again appears diminished by the central image of societal alienation and enslavement through systems of status and suppression: we are all victims of a social order that governs our existence. The role of God in salvation is likewise difficult to discern, appearing to be almost identified with the cutting edge of human social reform.

SALVATION IN THE NEW TESTAMENT

To try to summarize the roots in the New Testament of the under-standing of salvation that has been traditional in Christianity is also to risk considerable oversimplification. But some few points can be made by way of contrast to the alternative views sketched above. The first point is the most important, namely that the traditional understanding really does derive not from a philo-sophical analysis of the human condition or an ideological critique of society, but from the complex stories in the Bible itself. For this, Christians are indebted to Irenaeus of Lyons (late second century), who, in response to the speculations of the Gnostics, grounded orthodoxy in the narratives of the Old and New Testa-ments, showing that salvation was rooted in the history of a long relationship between humans and the God who created, called, chastised and finally graced them fully in the person of Jesus Christ.

The second point is that salvation involves the healing of a relationship between God and humans that only God can accom-plish. God alone saves. The implication of this is that both God and humans are *persons*, that is, they have the freedom to direct their knowing and love towards others. But declaring that God alone can save, that is, heal this relationship, implies also that human freedom is so enslaved by sin that it cannot direct itself properly. Sin is not a matter of the spirit being polluted by the body, nor is it a matter of people being enslaved by an unjust social order. It is a disease of freedom itself that is so profound, so complex, so entrenched, so *enslaved*, that only God – who has created us as free creatures – has power enough of knowledge and love to redirect that freedom rightly. Salvation is not about getting right knowledge of the self, nor about creating the right political order: it is about being in right relationship with God. And only God can make that relationship right.

JESUS AS SAVIOUR

If God above all is Saviour (Luke 1:47; 1 Tim. 1:1; 2:3, 4:10; Tit. 1:3; 3:4; Jude 25) and salvation comes from God (Luke 1:69, 71, 77; 3:6; Acts 28:28; Rom. 1:16; 10:1; 1 Thess. 5:9; 2 Thess. 2:13; 1 Pet. 1:5; Rev. 12:10), then the designation of Jesus in the New Testament as Saviour (*soter*) is of tremendous significance (see Luke 2:11; John 4:42; Acts 5:31; Eph. 5:23; Phil. 3:10; Tit. 1:4; 2:13; 2 Pet. 1:11; 2:10; 1 John 4:14). It means that God saves us through Jesus' agency. The New Testament has multiple ways of expressing this agency: Jesus is God's prophet (Luke 24:19; John 6:14), apostle (John 13:16), Word (John 1:1, 14) and, most frequently and intimately, God's Son (Matt 3:17; Mark 1:1; Luke 1:35; John 1:49; Rom. 1:3; 1 Cor. 1:9; Heb. 7:3; 1 John 1:3). Although the designation 'son' has obvious allusion to the relation of Israel with Yahweh (see Hos. 11:1; Matt. 2:15), when applied to Jesus it bears far deeper significance. It signifies not only that Jesus is the sort of human God desired, but also – and perhaps most of all – that Jesus was the very human face of God. The texts struggle to express this, saying variously that 'God sent his son' (Gal. 4:4) or 'God was with him' (Acts 10:38) or that 'God was in Christ reconciling the world to himself' (2 Cor. 5:19) or that the Word 'that was God' (John 1:1) also 'became flesh and dwelt among us' (John 1:14). It is on statements such as these that the dogma of the incarnation is grounded, a confession that orthodoxy has defended against all diminutions, for if *God* has not entered into the fabric of human freedom to heal it, then it remains unhealed.

But that same conviction also led to the insistence on the full *humanity* of Jesus, for if *human freedom* is not touched by God neither can the relationship between God and humans be healed. Jesus was not simply the 'human appearance' of the divine, as the docetists would have it, nor simply a fleshly vehicle for the divine word, as the Monophysites would have it. Jesus was 'born of a woman, born under the law' (Gal. 4:4). He lived a true human existence from the cradle to the grave. As Hebrews says: 'Since, therefore, the children share in flesh and blood, he himself likewise partook of the same nature, that through death he might destroy him who has the power of death, that is, the devil, and deliver all those who through fear of death were subject to lifelong bondage . . . because he himself has suffered and been tempted, he is able to help those who are tempted' (Heb. 2:14–15, 18). The implication is that precisely through the disposition of his human freedom, precisely through the *way* in which he was human, Jesus was Saviour. If the alienation of sin is spelled out in the disease of freedom that distorts the relationship with God and thus all other relationships as well in an ever-widening pattern that infects communities and societies so that they institutionalize the idolatrous impulses of the human heart (see Rom. 1:18–32), then the saving presence of Jesus must begin with the way in which his human freedom expressed the right relationship with God and thus all other relationships as well in an ever-widening pattern of healing and reconciliation reaching even to the structures of human society. Hebrews, again: 'When he came into the world he said, "Sacrifices and offerings thou hast not desired, but a body thou hast prepared for me; in burnt offerings and sin offerings thou has taken no pleasure. Then I said, 'Lo, I have come to do thy will, O God' . . ." And by that will, we have been sanctified through the offering of the body of Jesus Christ once for all' (Heb. 10:5–10; see Rom. 3:21–26).

For the writings of the New Testament, the words of Jesus do not by themselves save, even though 'no man ever spoke as this man' (John 8:48) and he had 'words of eternal life' (John 6:68). Nor do the deeds of Jesus by themselves save, even though they were deeds of healing and reconciliation, unless they were received in faith (see Luke 7:50; 8:50; 17:19 and Mark 6:5–6). More fundamental than words and deeds was the heart of the Saviour, his deepest orientation in the world, his most fundamental attitudes, in a word, the disposition of his freedom. Or, to put it another way, it was the *character* of Jesus the human person through which God brought salvation to all humans.

Despite the diversity of images for Jesus found in the New Testament compositions, they are remarkably consonant on their understanding of this character, Jesus' identity. He is understood as 'the righteous one' who lived by faith (see Luke 23:47; Acts 3:14; 7:52; Rom. 1:17; Gal. 3:11; Heb. 10:38; 1 John 1:9; 2:1), and who found the right directing of human freedom in the most radical obedience to the living God (Rom. 5:12–21). That faithful obedience, in turn, was expressed by his faithful self-donation to his fellow humans. He is, simply, the one 'who gave himself' (Mark 10:45; Gal. 1:4; 2:20; Eph. 5:1, 25: Tit. 2:14). The identity of Jesus was given its perfect and final expression by his death, which was not only the ultimate act of obedience to God (Mark 14:36; Phil. 2:5–11), but also the ultimate expression of love towards others, 'for the son of Man did not come to be served but to serve and to give his life as a ransom for many' (Mark 10:45). By thus becoming 'the pioneer and perfecter of faith' (Heb. 12:2), Jesus was himself perfected as the human Son of God, and 'became the source of eternal salvation to all who obey him' (Heb. 5:9; see Acts 4:12).

FOR US AND FOR OUR SALVATION

The New Testament speaks of Jesus as 'mediator' (1 Tim. 2:5; Heb. 8:6; 9:15; 12:24) because in him God's offer of salvation and the human acceptance of salvation are joined. Paul says, 'The Son of God, Jesus Christ, whom we preached among you, Silvanus and Timothy and I, was not Yes and No; but in him it is always

Yes. For all the promises of God find their Yes in him. That is why we utter the Amen through him, to the glory of God' (2 Cor. 1:19–20). Through the Resurrection, the power of God at work in Jesus during his human life, 'reconciling the world to himself' (2 Cor. 5:19), was poured out abundantly on others, enabling them to have the same 'faith that saves' that was distinctive to Jesus, for 'God has put his seal on us and given us his Spirit as a guarantee' (2 Cor. 1:22). Those who live by this Spirit of Jesus, also walk by this Spirit (Gal. 5:16, 25), which means living according to the character revealed by Jesus: 'Bear one another's burdens and so fulfil the law of Christ' (Gal. 6:2).

How does Jesus save us according to the New Testament? Not by freeing our souls from our bodies, or by adjusting the arrangements of society, but by transforming human freedom so that we can be in right relationship with God and with each other. Since salvation in this tradition is relational, it cannot remain private; to be in right relationship with God demands also to be in right relationship with the world, beginning in communities that live by 'the mind of Christ' (1 Cor. 2:16; Phil. 2:5), which means that 'each one looks not only to his own interests but also to the interests of others' (Phil. 2:4). The classic Christian tradition has understood this to mean living out the identity of Jesus within a Church that takes seriously 'walking in love as Christ loved us and gave himself up for us' (Eph. 5:2).

In short, the Catholic understanding of salvation does not see it in oversimplified terms as either a flight from the world or a restructuring of the world, but in terms of the patient living through of complex life together in the world. Just as Jesus shows us a God who saves all humans by entering fully into the fabric of a highly particular human existence, defined and constrained by a specific time and place, and just as Jesus shows us a brother whose faith in God and love for others reveals the right direction of human freedom played out in the tangled web of difficult and intractable social realities, so are those who live 'by the faith of the Son of God who loved us and gave himself for us' (Gal. 2:20) convinced by Paul's words that 'with fear and trembling you are working out your salvation, for God is at work in you, both to will and to work for his good pleasure' (Phil. 2:13).

And by so living, we dwell in hope of a future salvation as well (Rom. 8:24): 'Our commonwealth is in heaven, and from it we await a saviour, the Lord Jesus Christ, who will change our lowly body to be like his glorious body, by the power which enables him even to subject all things to himself' (Phil. 3:20). As we now say 'Amen' to the Father through him in the assembly (2 Cor. 1:20), we also long for the day when, as he came to be with us in our sorrow, we will be with him in God's joy (see 1 Thess. 4:13–18).